6

The Disease Concept Applied to Psychiatric Conditions without Known Neuropathologies

There are psychiatric conditions for which the disease concept is deemed apt but which can as yet be described only as clinical syndromes that remain unvalidated by the discernment of underlying pathological entities or etiological agencies. When faced with such conditions we must be clear about our terminology, not only because we lack the corrective and confirming influences of morbid anatomy and physiology but also because we must depend, to a degree that is disconcerting in modern medicine, on our skill at differentiating mental experiences one from another and at evaluating their significance and relationship to the course of illness. Here more than elsewhere our reasoning and its terminology can lead us astray.

Many patients who consult psychiatrists come because new, disturbing, and uncontrollable mental experiences have intruded into their lives. It appears as though a process expressed in moods, thoughts, or perceptions has disrupted what had for them been an integrated system of capacities and emotions. This process has rendered many of their psychological experiences ineffective or alien. Some of these patients, who also demonstrate paralyses or sensory losses, can be recognized as suffering from pathological conditions that disrupt brain function, and we appreciate their mental changes as other symptoms of that pathology. But there are also patients with similar mental symptoms for which a clear pathology cannot be found. What of them? In the absence of demonstrable somatic change, why use the disease concept rather than another?

Disease denotes disruptions of the organism and of some part of it in particular. In general medicine the symptoms indicative of disruption are the appearance of something unusual, such as pain, or the disablement of some natural function, such as temperature control (fever). Similarly, in psychiatry the construal of a disease is prompted by evidence of the breakdown of normal capacities, such as intelligence and consciousness, or by the appearance of new forms of mental phenomena, such as hallucinations (perceptions without stimuli) or delusions (fixed, false, idiosyncratic beliefs).

Again, in using the term *form* we refer to particular kinds of mental activity, such as thinking, dreaming, perceiving, and calculating, as well as to the connections linking perceptions with emotions or one thought with another. All of these "forms," or kinds of mental activity, can be usefully distinguished from their "content," that is, what the individual is dreaming or thinking about or what specific perceptions led to what particular emotional response.

Although many people seek psychiatric attention because of a disturbance in mental content (for example, demoralization after failure or anxiety with uncertainty), it is the patient with new and unusual forms of mental experience that is most in need of an explanation that goes beyond our appreciation of him as a distressed subject. Thus, if his disturbance takes the form of hallucinations, regardless of what the patient hallucinates about, his experience of perceptions without stimuli must be explained. Other disruptions in the form of mental life include delusions, the loss of connections between thoughts (formal thought disorder), and disturbances in the congruity of mood and behavior. The opinion that these phenomena represent symptoms derived from disorders in the organism is quite compelling, especially since identical phenomena are provoked by conditions whose origin in brain dysfunction has been discovered.

These changes in the forms of mental life are often called psychotic phenomena, and the conditions in which they occur are called the psychoses. But *psychosis* and *psychotic* are terms intended simply to indicate that mental life has been disrupted in its capacities or forms; they are ambiguous as to the degree and kind of that disruption. In this way, *psychosis* is the modern equivalent of *insanity,* which had itself replaced *lunacy* in professional and polite usage. Each of these words indicates the disruption of mental life by a process that brings new forms of psychological experience.

The term *psychosis* is thus broadly categorical and includes subgroups within it. Dementia and delirium are psychoses because they are characterized by disturbances in intellectual capacity and consciousness. Affective disorder and schizophrenia are psychoses because they disrupt the form of mental life with incomprehensible moods, delusions, and hallucinations.

Occasionally the term *psychosis* is given a more special meaning, a practice that can be deplored because it usually renders vague what could, with specific terminology, be clear. Thus, *psychotic* may be taken as a synonym for *schizophrenic,* though the latter term is to be preferred because there are many psychotic individuals (the delirious, the manic, etc.) who are not schizophrenic. When used instead of *delusional* or *hallucinated, psychotic* obscures important differences in psychopathology. Finally, the term *psychotic* can be employed to mean intensely disturbed. This usage often carries the hidden theoretical implication that all mental difficulties are a continuum, with neurotic states approaching and becoming psychotic ones as disturbance increases. If *psychosis* is merely a synonym for *severity,* however, the distinctions possible between categories of disorder may be lost, and with them clues to mechanism and etiology.

In the next chapters we will discuss those conditions that appear with incomprehensible moods, delusions, or hallucinations and as yet lack an adequate explanation. These syndromes, manic-depressive illness and schizophrenia, are often called "functional" psychoses (this use of *function* must be distinguished from our concept of function as the purpose and meaning of mental events and behaviors in an individual's life). These "functional" psychoses are contrasted with "organic" ones, like delirium and dementia, in which pathological mechanisms and etiological agencies have been demonstrated.) Psychiatric syndromes with and without recognized brain disease were noted in 1758 by William Battie, who wrote of "consequential" and "Original" madness:

> First then, there is some reason to fear that Madness is Original, when it neither follows nor accompanies any accident, which may justly be deemed its external and remoter cause. Secondly, there is more reason to fear that, whenever this disorder is hæreditary, it is Original. For, altho' even in such case it may now and then be excited by some external and known cause, yet the striking oddities that characterise whole families derived from Lunatic ancestors, and the frequent breaking forth of real Madness in the offspring of such illconcerted alliances, and that from little or no provocation, strongly intimate that the nerves or instruments of Sensation in such persons are not originally formed perfect and like the nerves of other men. Thirdly, we may with the greatest degree of probability affirm that Madness is Original, when it both ceases and appears afresh without any assignable cause . . . Original Madness, whether it be hæreditary or intermitting, is not removable by any method, which the science of Physick in its present imperfect state is able to suggest. But altho' Original Madness is never radically cured by human art, its ill-conditioned fate is however a little recompensed sometimes by a perfect recovery, sometimes by long intervals of sanity, without our assistance and beyond our expectation. Besides Original Madness is in itself very little prejudicial to animal life . . . Madness, which is consequential to other disorders or external causes, altho' it now and then admits of relief by the removal or correction of such disorders or causes; yet in proportion to the force and continued action of such causes, and according to the circumstances of the preceding disorders, it is very often complicated with many other ill effects of those causes and disorders; and, tho' it may not in itself be prejudicial to bodily health, any more than Original Madness, yet by its companions it becomes fatal or greatly detrimental to animal life [53].

That manic-depressive illness and schizophrenia share many attributes of Battie's "Original Madness" is clear, but in calling them functional as opposed to organic disorders we should be wary not to conclude that a neuropathology is nonexistent or that these disorders are produced by some disturbance in the integrative "functioning" of the brain or mind, perhaps entirely caused by psychological factors. *Cryptogenic* or *idiopathic* might be better adjectives than *functional,* for manic-depressive illness and schizophrenia are major mysteries in medicine. They are mysterious because, though they provoke dramatic and disabling symptoms, we know little about their causes or mechanisms. We can recognize them, predict something of their course, and symptomatically treat patients with empirically derived methods, but neither rational therapy nor prevention is yet possible. The relative stereotypy of symptoms and course has prompted application of the disease concept to their study, but manic-depressive illness and schizophrenia so far remain clinical entities without pathological mechanisms or etiological agencies that can be confidently assigned.

As a brief historical review will make apparent, even the recognition and differentiation of these conditions have been problematic.

A Historical Note on
Manic-depressive Disorder and Schizophrenia

The histories of the concepts of manic-depressive disorder and schizophrenia are inextricably entwined. It is impossible to write of one and not the other, and it is difficult to avoid turning a background note on these conditions into a history of psychiatry.

It is common teaching that Emil Kraepelin first separated manic-depressive disorder and schizophrenia. The earlier masters—Pinel, Esquirol, Griesinger, and Maudsley—did, however, recognize two clinical aspects of severe insanity: one characterized by disturbed emotions (affectional insanity), the other by disturbed thoughts and beliefs without a prominent change in mood (ideational insanity). These men taught that affectional insanity tended to have a periodic character in which depressed and exalted moods could alternate and that it might completely remit, but they also held that many patients with affectional insanity would go on to develop ideational insanity as the second stage of an illness then appearing in its incurable guise. Griesinger was particularly insistent in his opinion that insanity is one disorder with several stages (*Einheitpsychose*), in which the affective disorder constitutes the first and recoverable form and the ideational illness appears "only as consequences and terminations of the first when the cerebral affection has not been cured" [54].

Griesinger, whose 1845 text, *Mental Pathology and Therapeutics,* can still be read with pleasure, divided insanity into melancholia, mania, monomania, and dementia, any one of which could be partial or complete. Each of these was conceived of as a symptom cluster that the disease—insanity—could assume at different periods in its course, although every patient did not experience the whole course in this way. With this approach Griesinger hoped to avoid a meaningless proliferation of psychiatric entities based on individual cases.

But Griesinger and his contemporaries were misled by their inability to extricate the syphilitic condition, general paresis, from the population of insane patients. The succession of stages from early affective change through to dementia in general paresis provided Griesinger with examples in which symptoms of altered mood began the illness and then gave way to delusions and dementia, with death as the inevitable consequence. Advances in neuropathology were needed before this sequence of symptoms could be recognized as distinct from that found in other mental disorders.

Confidence in the unitary view of insanity was shattered when general paresis was distinguished. Here was a clearly recognizable disease, which followed many of the steps that Griesinger had described but in which a regular neuropathology (chronic meningoencephalitis) and a distinct etiology (syphilitic infection) could be determined. This nineteenth- and early twentieth-century advance depended upon the combination of epidemiological considerations, clinicopathological correlations, and eventually on serological and bacteriological identification.

The French psychiatrists Falret and Baillarger, concentrating on "affective insanity," further crippled the concept of a unitary condition by describing remissions and relapses in the course of melancholic and manic conditions that they called *folie circulaire* or *folie à doubleforme.* They documented that this intermittent insanity did not end in a continuous illness but was characterized by periods, some apparently permanent, in which full health was restored.

Kraepelin recognized the implications of these developments for concepts of mental illness, particularly the one he labeled *manic-depressive insanity,* a term used to include under one disease entity circular insanities, simple manias, melancholia, and even those conditions in which more minor disturbances in mood occurred in a periodic or continuous way without obvious relationship to a patient's experiences[55]. The common bond he saw in all forms of this entity was a uniform prognosis: manic-depressive insanity never led to a profound deterioration of personality or thinking, not even when attacks continued for many years. Rather, all morbid manifestations could completely disappear, either between attacks or permanently after a series of them.

Kraepelin distinguished manic-depressive insanity from the condition he called *dementia praecox,* a term first used by the French psychiatrist Benoît Morel. In this syndrome, Kraepelin recognized a variety of states in which a disturbance in thinking, emotion, and volition led eventually to a destruction of the personality peculiar to this condition itself.

Kraepelin's conception of these psychoses was heuristically valuable. It focused attention on a salient feature of mental illness—that some patients recover and others deteriorate—and it encouraged genetic studies to discover whether the heredities of these conditions were as distinct as their courses. Finally, it led Kraepelin and others to attempt to define symptoms that would distinguish the two conditions prior to the fulfillment of their prognoses. Such efforts continue to this day.

Defining and prognosticating are unsatisfactory activities for physicians if they do not lead either to an understanding of causes or to effective treatment. The failure to discover a treatment that could change the course of either manic-depressive insanity or dementia praecox caused Kraepelin's concepts to be challenged.

Eugen Bleuler sought to further the Kraepelinian advance by examining dementia praecox for a central, defining feature. He coined the word *schizophrenia* for the condition, presumed there might be many etiologies for the disorder (and thus spoke of the "group of schizophrenias"), and attempted to explain its symptoms as the result of some fundamental defect in the capacity of the mind to unify thought processes and mental events[56]. Bleuler's term *schizophrenia* has stayed with the condition, probably because the word *dementia* is used in another context and because not all patients develop the illness while young. Since thinking is disrupted in so many situations, however, Bleuler's emphasis on thought disorder as central to schizophrenia and his desire to recognize cases in their earliest and subtlest manifestations perhaps led him and his followers to diagnose the illness more often than Kraepelin would have done.

The major quarrels with Kraepelinian opinion that have characterized psychiatry in the twentieth century have had less to do with distinctions between manic-depressive disorder and schizophrenia than with the issue of whether or not such conditions are best conceptualized as diseases. Are they disorders qualitatively distinct from states of mental health and produced by the action of some biological agent leading to disruption of neural and thus mental function? or are they more correctly viewed as reactions to life experiences in which people differ from one another only in their degree of response?

Several physicians have looked for functional explanations of these psychoses through an appreciation of the life experiences and mental conflicts of their patients. Sigmund Freud published his studies of manic-depressive disorder and schizophrenia only after his initial psychoanalytic work, perhaps because he began as a neurologist in private practice and was involved primarily in the treatment of neurotic patients. In fact, his major study of schizophrenia, the Schreber case, was based on Schreber's published autobiography rather than on a personal examination[57]. Freud concentrated his attention on the contents of Schreber's delusions and derived a functional explanation of paranoid schizophrenia from the subject's conflicts, particularly those over homosexuality. Freud ignored the form of the delusional experiences and did not discuss how his opinions could account for the deteriorating course of the illness. But his meaningful explanations have survived, not only because he founded the psychoanalytic movement but perhaps because he brought an encouraging and humane view of schizophrenic patients to physicians who had to treat them through long periods of therapeutic impotence. The same view can be taken of Freud's attempt in "Mourning and Melancholia" to explain the symptoms of affective disorder[58].

Adolf Meyer likewise characterized manic-depressive disorder and schizophrenia as reactions rather than as diseases[59]. He encouraged the study of a patient's biography so as to see the condition as an outcome of the patient's whole life experience. Again, Meyer's opinions had the advantage of explaining disorder as derived from issues best resolved through an understanding of the patient's psychological needs and assets; but he also ignored the necessity for such theories to account for the form of symptoms and their natural history. His view, like Freud's, rested primarily on the plausibility of his explanations.

Karl Jaspers was the first to make the point that it might be difficult to choose a single position in such a controversy, since similar psychological events might be produced by circumstances in some patients and by disease in others. He demonstrated this in a study of what has been called morbid jealousy, pointing out that the symptom sometimes appears in individuals in whom a lifelong trait of suspiciousness has understandably progressed, owing to circumstances, into unfounded excessive jealousy (for which we might use the term *neurotic jealousy*), whereas in other patients the symptom appears unanticipated by the previous personality and unrelated to life events—it seems incomprehensible, a delusion with jealousy as its content[60]. It was this incomprehensibility that Jaspers concluded to be characteristic of schizophrenic symptoms, and, as his terms *life break* and *process phenomena* indicate, he believed that such symptoms reflected the interruption of coherent mental life and behavior by a somatic disorder. Since the psychopathology of manic-depressive illness is also incomprehensible in its form, however, it is difficult to hold with Jaspers that such a characteristic is limited to schizophrenic symptoms.

Attempts to see these conditions always as reactions have lost momentum in the last few years with the appearance of symptomatic treatments for manic-depressive disorder and schizophrenia and with the recognition of similar conditions that are produced by agents that affect the brain. But the continuing failure to identify a particular cerebral pathology or pathophysiology in these disorders undermines attempts to proclaim them as diseases with complete confidence. They remain mysteries in the sense that a comprehension of their essential nature is lacking. They seem best viewed as clinical entities for which no certain pathological entities or etiological agencies have as yet been discovered. We are fortunate to have chanced upon treatments that help, and in that regard we perhaps resemble Withering after his discovery of digitalis—grateful but astonished.

7

The Manic-Depressive Syndrome: A Disorder in the Affective Realm

It is natural to consider changes in moods and emotions to occur in relation to life's events and the capacity for such affective responses to be a normal human characteristic. This affective capacity is disrupted in manic-depressive illness, hence the alternative diagnostic term, *affective disorder.* Disruption in the regulation of affect is the fundamental symptom justifying the application of the disease concept to this condition despite the absence of demonstrable neuropathology.

The terms *affect, affective,* and *affectivity* deserve some further consideration. *Affect* is defined by Webster as "feeling, emotion and desire with an implication of their importance in determining thought and conduct." Psychiatrists, following Bleuler's lead, have identified an affective as distinct from a cognitive realm of mental life. These two aspects of mind relate to each other, but it is not difficult to appreciate that thoughts, reasons, perceptions, and thinking are different from moods, emotions, drives, and feeling.

In normal mental life there is a coherent and natural relationship between these two domains. Most thoughts are accompanied by some feeling tone, and certain thoughts can produce strong emotions, such as grief. In a similar way, most moods are associated with particular thoughts, as when fear leads to suspicion. That a distinction between the cognitive and affective realms is not made arbitrarily and can reveal an important aspect of mental organization is corroborated by the existence of a class of disorders that strikes primarily at the affective aspect of mental life and produces profound alterations in moods, emotions, and drives.

Affect is a broad term encompassing moods, emotions, motivations, and such feelings as pleasure, confidence, depression, and discouragement. Attempts to replace it with other words are usually unsatisfactory. *Mood* describes a relatively persistent, dominating affect; *emotions* are more fleeting

53

affective events; and *feeling* is a word confused with bodily sensation. The term *affect* is needed because it encompasses this whole sphere of psychic life; for this reason, the phrase *affective disorder* often replaces *mood disorder* or *manic-depressive disorder*. The sense that some primary disruption has occurred in the affective realm is the critical premise in the category.

Manic-depressive illness can be viewed as a clinical syndrome and is thus most easily defined as it is described—by its symptoms and course. The symptom cluster that characterizes the disorder consists of three related and reliably elicited mental changes: a disturbance in mood, a change in self-attitude, and a subjective sense of alteration in mental energy and bodily health.

The course of manic-depressive illness is one of remissions and relapses, the syndrome usually appearing in an unpredictable fashion and persisting for a variable duration. Each episode, even if untreated, eventually abates, and the patient is restored to his premorbid, symptom-free condition until the next attack.

The most striking feature of this course is that polar distinctions may occur in the affective qualities of different episodes. With some attacks the mood is depressive in character, whereas with others it is elated. There is individual variety in this feature. Some patients can alternate from depression to elation in successive episodes. Others may show a preponderance of one mood state over the other or throughout their illness have attacks only of mania or only of depression. However, it is the tendency of many patients to have attacks in both modes that has led to the designation manic-depressive disorder.

The shift in mood toward either depression or elation/excitement is the clearest of the disorder's characteristic features, and the diagnosis of manic-depressive illness should not be made without it. Patients are often able to distinguish this pathological and uncontrollable mood change from ordinary emotional reactions, and they comment about its odd and pervasive quality, its unremitting nature, and its similarity from one attack to another. Although such patients have previously felt sad and happy in response to life events, the mood during these episodes, whether of misery or ecstasy, often feels qualitatively different from those prior experiences. Many patients can promptly recognize a recurrence of their illness because of this special and quite characteristic change in mood, although its severity may vary with each attack.

The affective change is experienced in many other features of mental life. When depressed, the patient becomes withdrawn and loses interest in most activities, including those that usually give him pleasure and comfort. Even his perceptions of the environment may become dulled, and he can report that sounds are muffled, colors faded or darkened, and food tasteless. Just the opposite happens in mania, when social and other activities increase and when perceptions can become brighter and more intense. In whatever terms these changes are described, the critical feature is that the patient's mood is fixed in one direction or the other. The primary psychological disturbance produced by this clinical entity is a shift in mood that takes on a sustained character, one that, especially in the depressive phase of the illness, is little influenced by life events. Mood, usually a responsive feature of mental life, here acts in an uncontrollable and independent fashion.

A second symptom is the change in self-attitude that usually parallels the change in mood and is in some sense hard to differentiate from the mood itself. The manic patient may believe that he is healthy, rich, talented, or powerful, although, when depressed, he may feel diseased, poor, blameworthy, or useless. Such changes in self-attitude are often delusional. In the depressed phase, the patient can thus take on the view that he is a notorious criminal, that he is infected with venereal disease or filled with cancer, and that he deserves public humiliation or death. In mania, on the other hand, the patient may believe that he is God, that he is a millionaire, or that he has the knowledge and powers to save mankind. With these delusions and as elaborations of them, the patient may think that others are trying to harm him. Such delusions are felt by the patient to be deserved (as a just punishment for his terrible crimes or as the products of envy for his extraordinary powers, for example), a characteristic that can sometimes help to distinguish the persecutory beliefs of affective disorder from those of paranoid schizophrenia, in which the patient usually believes others to be oppressing him without justification.

Such delusional changes in self-attitude may prompt destructive behavior. The fear and shame derived from delusions of blameworthiness can lead the depressed patient to suicide and even to family homicide if he believes that his relatives are tainted with or face humiliation because of his evil. In mania, a delusional belief in personal wealth may culminate in overspending to the point of financial ruin.

A change in the patient's sense of mental energy and bodily health is the third characteristic symptom of manic-depressive illness. In the depressed phase of the disorder his thinking may be slow and inefficient and he may complain of fatigue or physical discomfort. These features are also evident on examination, and the patient can appear ill and apathetic, with demonstrable deficits in his abilities to concentrate and to perform mental tasks. When seen in more severe form all aspects of the patient's mental and physical activity are slowed. He displays a remarkable psychomotor retardation, answering slowly if at all and walking with a gait, posture, rigidity, and facial expression suggestive of Parkinsonism. A stuporous condition is the most severe manifestation of this phenomenon, with the patient bedridden, incontinent, mute, unable to feed or care for himself, and in danger of death if not properly diagnosed and treated.

In the manic state, on the other hand, the patient may experience his thoughts as effortless and rapid and his body as healthy and filled with energy. As this condition worsens, the patient may become progressively more active until his behavior takes on an uncontrollable driven quality and his thoughts become so rapid and chaotically responsive to every distraction that sustained, goal-directed thinking is impossible.

This central cluster of symptoms is often accompanied by a variety of affect-related complaints. Motivated behaviors, for example, are altered during the illness, usually in a direction congruent with mood, self-attitude, and sense of energy. In the depressed phase, a patient usually has little appetite, loses weight, sleeps poorly, and is uninterested in sex. During a manic attack, however, the same patient may eat and drink with enthusiasm, sleep little but be refreshed by it, and experience such an increase in sexual energy that both family relationships and social reputation are endangered. Patients may also describe a diurnal variation in mood and sense of vitality; for example, mornings are classically the worst time of day for patients during the depressive phase of the disorder.

As in the other conditions for which the disease concept seems appropriate, patients may experience hallucinations and manifest disordered thought. The hallucinations (usually auditory or visual in form) almost always take as their content themes that are understandable in light of the mood change; manic patients may hear the voice of God praising their actions, whereas depressed patients may see distressing scenes of their relatives being tortured. Thought disorder is rare in the depressed phase of the illness, but its occurrence in mania is not uncommon, with pressured speech, rhymes, puns, and rapid change of topic occasionally progressing to illogical and incoherent speech [61].

The course of manic-depressive illness can be episodic, periodic, or cyclical. A few patients suffer only a single attack (usually depression) during their lifetime, whereas others have repeated bouts of depression, mania and depression, or, least commonly, mania alone. In most episodes, attacks occur unpredictably, though both psychological and physical stresses can precipitate them; women who experience the disorder may be at special risk in the post-partum state. The illness can also appear in a periodic fashion, with patients regularly becoming ill in fall or spring. The reason for this seasonal variation is unknown, but it may be tied to some biological oscillatory mechanism with a long period, such as is found in hibernating animals. Finally, in a small number of patients, the disorder may take a cyclical course, with attacks of mania and depression following one another in a regular sequence. In such cases there may be a predictable change from mania to depression and back again every forty-eight hours[62]. The occurrence of these regular cycles supports the opinion that biological mechanisms and etiologies lie at the root of the illness.

Possible Mechanisms and Etiologies of the Manic-Depressive Syndrome: The Process of Validation

The presumption that manic-depressive disorder is a disease is a construct in all the senses described in chapter 1. This presumption carries the implication that some as-yet-undemonstrated pathological mechanisms and etiological agencies will emerge to explain the stereotyped set of symptoms and consistent features of course that are represented in the clinical syndrome. Such discoveries, if they occur, will validate the construct as well as increase our therapeutic and prognostic abilities, and manic-depressive disorder will join dementia, delirium, Korsakoff's syndrome, and aphasia as a confirmed clinical disease entity.

The available data on which the validation for the construct manic-depressive illness rests, although indirect and fragmentary, are strong enough to give us confidence that the disease model will be found suitable. One important piece of evidence is the finding that the typical symptom cluster and even the bipolar course of manic-depressive illness can occur in other disorders that have known brain pathology. Patients with Huntington's disease, for example, may have, as their first symptom, depression or mania[63], and depressions indistinguishable from those in spontaneously arising manic-depressive illness can occur in the course of Cushing's syndrome and hypothyroidism[64]. The implication of these observations is that the affective syndrome, like dementia and delirium, is at least a potential reaction of a damaged brain, though for spontaneously arising manic-depressive illness the necessary and sufficient conditions provoking it are unknown. We can refer to manic-depressive syndromes occurring in the setting of known pathology as symptomatic in nature and can contrast them with the idiopathic disorder. This mode of reasoning is analogous to that for epilepsy, in which we distinguish seizures symptomatic of particular brain diseases from idiopathic epilepsy, in which genetic factors are important.

Current investigations about pathological mechanisms in manic-depressive illness are focused on the role of cerebral neurotransmitters. This area of research began in the 1950s with the clinical observation that reserpine, a drug used to treat hypertension, could produce a classical depressive syndrome[65]. Next, animal studies demonstrated that reserpine depleted brain stores of the neurotransmitters serotonin, norepinephrine, and dopamine. Thereafter the empirical discovery was made that monoamine oxidase inhibitors and tricyclic compounds not only reverse depressive syndromes but increase brain concentrations of the very neurotransmitters depleted by reserpine[66]. If reduction and increase of brain amines can produce depression and its reversal, might not this be the mechanism through which genetic and other etiological agencies cause the spontaneously arising disorder?

Genetic factors have in fact been proposed to play an etiological role in manic-depressive illness. Thus, in 1953, Kallmann demonstrated an increasing risk for manic-depressive illness in the relatives of patients hospitalized with the disorder [67]. He found rates of 16.7 percent for half-siblings, 22.7 percent for full siblings, 25.5 percent for dizygotic, or fraternal, twins (like full siblings), and 100 percent for monozygotic, or identical, twins. Although subsequent studies using different diagnostic procedures and sampling techniques have found somewhat different results (for example, higher risk for full siblings and less-than-perfect concordance in monozygotic twins), there is general agreement that a genetic, and hence biological, factor is implicated in the pathogenesis of many cases of bipolar manic-depressive illness.

It can be argued that environmental rather than genetic causes are responsible for the findings of these family studies and that, for example, increasing similarity of upbringing could account for the greater concordance rates in monozygotic as opposed to dizygotic twins and in full siblings compared with half-siblings. In some pedigrees of manic-depressive illness, however, a clear-cut genetic transmission has been shown, with the affective syndrome closely linked to a known genetic marker (that for color blindness) on the short arm of the X chromosome[68]. This again suggests that spontaneously arising manic-depressive illness can be the expression of a disordered biology for which the disease concept is an appropriate conceptual model.

There have been other observations suggesting a biological etiology for manic-depressive illness, including the finding that a drug of abuse (phencyclidine) can induce a typical manic state[69] and that antidepressant treatment of depressed patients may precipitate mania[70]. Although we have not discovered the pathological disease entities and etiological agencies responsible for most cases of manic-depressive illness, the best way to integrate data from symptomatic illnesses, neurotransmitter studies, genetics, and other areas of inquiry appears to be the stepwise process of reasoning from the disease model. A conjunctive category is emerging in the study of this condition, which can be viewed as a disorder of the affective mechanisms of the brain. These affective mechanisms are now the subject of investigation and may reveal the structural substrate to confirm and consolidate the conjunction.

In summary, the pathognomonic feature of the manic-depressive syndrome is the deregulation of the affective domain of mental life, resulting in an unrestrained dominance of mental activity by affect. Its construal as a disease would be validated if we had a pathophysiology of affect. Such a validating advance in neuroscience could also explain the natural history of the syndrome, its distinction from affective reactions such as grief, and its response to symptomatic treatments.

8

The Schizophrenic Syndrome

[handwritten annotations: "unifying psychological feature to the given condition as a construct" and "validation of as a construct"]

Psychiatrists have difficulty agreeing on a definition of schizophrenia. This is not only because its characteristics are mental changes lacking a defined pathology that can be separately observed, for such is also true of manic-depressive disorder. More important, schizophrenia does not have a unifying psychological feature that can be regarded as both fundamental to the condition and necessary for its recognition. Even at the clinical level it lacks a clear point of reference for validating it as a construct. There can be no diagnosis of dementia without a decline in intelligence, of delirium without alteration in consciousness, or of manic-depressive illness without change in affectivity; in schizophrenia there is no such central characteristic. Because it is a disjunctive category with a vengeance, not all writers on the subject of schizophrenia will be talking about the same type of patient or even about the same condition. A discussion of schizophrenia must begin with a long clinical description, which is the only form of definition anyone can so far provide.

Our definition would describe schizophrenia as a clinical syndrome distinguished from others by its symptoms and natural history. Its course is not uniform. Schizophrenia can appear insidiously and progress slowly and relentlessly or it can begin suddenly and continue with exacerbations and remissions. The most dramatic features occur during active phases of the disorder and take the form of hallucinations and delusions. Odd modes of thinking, peculiar incongruities of mood, and a loss of mental energy varying from minimal to severe can develop gradually or during an acute attack, and all of these signs and symptoms may remain after an exacerbation, to worsen with subsequent ones. The disorder often renders the patient's personality cold and unpredictable, and it may lead to a disappearance of his finer sensibilities and capacities for affection. It is a devastating disturbance of mental life and behavior which appears in its basic guise without evidence of coarse brain disease and in the absence of a primary change in mood or self-attitude.

Schizophrenia usually begins in late adolescence or young adult life, although onset even after sixty also occurs. In general, the illness produces a deterioration of personality, so that even if delusions, hallucinations, and thought disorder abate, patients often remain intellectually and emotionally crippled, with poverty of thought, a narrowed range of interests, and a life isolated from family and friends. Deterioration is not inevitable, however, for even before the discovery of neuroleptic drugs remissions were reported in ten to twenty-five percent of cases, a figure that could be improved with effective treatments and programs of social rehabilitation.

Among the signs and symptoms that mark the onset of a schizophrenic illness, none can be agreed on as characteristic of the disorder. Emotional unrest, uncertainty, and perplexity can be found in many conditions, so the diagnosis of schizophrenia cannot rest on them alone. As Kurt Schneider pointed out, however, a number of mental changes are found more often in schizophrenia than in the other disorders. These phenomena can usefully be divided into abnormal mental experiences and disturbed modes of expression[71]. The abnormal mental experiences, which Schneider referred to as "first rank symptoms," are better evidence of the illness only because they are more reliably elicited and are less dependent on observers' interpretations than are the changes in expression.

Abnormal Mental Experiences in Schizophrenia

Hallucinations and delusions are the most vivid schizophrenic mental experiences, though it must be remembered that these symptoms also occur in delirium, dementia, and manic-depressive illness. Although hallucinations can arise in any sensory modality, auditory hallucinations are commonest, and in the absence of affective disorder or coarse brain disease certain types of auditory hallucinations are almost diagnostic of schizophrenia. Thus, the patient who hears voices arguing with one another (often referring to him in the third person), voices commenting on his every action, or voices repeating his thoughts (*Gedankenlautwerden; echo des pensées*) experiences hallucinations most typical of schizophrenia.

Delusions in schizophrenia can begin as vague, fearful interpretations or "half-beliefs" and then develop into incorrigible convictions that are well formed and persistent. A delusion coming on suddenly, not prompted by a hallucination or previous delusion and not related in any obvious way to the patient's mood, is called a primary or autochthonous delusion and is highly suggestive of schizophrenia.

Many other characteristic schizophrenic experiences are of delusional form but have such individual features that they have been named separately. In one, somatic passivity, the patient ascribes bodily sensations to some external agency. The sensation may be rooted in an obvious physical process or in a hallucination. A patient of Mellor's had injured his right knee in a fall, but reported: "The sun-rays are directed by a U.S. army satellite in an intense beam which I can feel entering the centre of my knee and then radiating outwards causing the pain"[72]. In all of these phenomena the patient is unwillingly subjected to experiences that seem completely real to him and that terrify or perplex him. It is the inexplicability of these phenomena which has led to consideration of them as symptoms of disease.

Disturbed Modes of Expression in Schizophrenia

In contrast to these abnormal experiences are disturbances in the patient's mode of expression. One such disturbance, though present in other disorders and absent in many schizophrenic patients, is an abnormality of thought characterized by vagueness and the lack of relationship between one idea and another. The name given this abnormality—thought disorder—refers to a disturbance in the form of the patient's thought rather than in its content. It is the relationship of ideas to one another that is abnormal in thought disorder rather than the truth or falsity of a given thought. An example of this phenomenon is provided by Slater and Roth, whose patient, in a passage reminiscent of the speech of fluent aphasia, wrote:

> It is a tragedy perhaps, I find practically all the foriegn human beings had this knowledge, and perhaps at least certain of our own Nationality such as myself had not, even my friends, comrades, where aware as the State Authoraties must have been, which I feel you will accept as to be STs—in all aspects revalent to delibe-rary to try and induce, such as been my lot, constant body, head, Activation numerical strong, and distance Voice face and body barrage[73].

Thought disorder, like other abnormalities of expression, is a disturbance to be described in dimensional rather than categorical terms. Thus, whereas patients are either hallucinating or not (a categorical distinction), the expression of their thoughts can be ranged along a continuum from logical and goal-directed to irrelevant and incoherent. Difficulty in recognizing thought disorder comes not at the extremes of this dimension but in the middle, where one examiner's threshold for vagueness may be different from another's and where the effects of culture and facility in language may be difficult to appreciate. Disturbed modes of expression are less reliably rated than are abnormal mental experiences[10]. The latter, which can be judged either present or absent and about which patients can be asked, should receive greater weight in the diagnostic process.

Disturbance is also sometimes seen in the patient's emotional expression. Early in the illness he may appear inexplicably angry, perplexed, or ecstatic, and although questioning usually reveals that such feelings are due to delusions or hallucinations, at times the patient is unable to account for them. His emotional state may also seem incongruous to the thoughts he is expressing; thus, he may laugh while saying he is miserable and frightened. Finally, and especially after the acute symptoms have subsided, the patient may be uncharacteristically cold and distant, whatever the circumstances. These disturbances in emotional expression may be the patient's most disconcerting symptom and even when mild can be baffling and distressing to his family.

Other abnormal modes of expression occasionally found in schizophrenia are those disturbances in activity, posture, and mobility called catatonic symptoms. (Again it is important to note that such symptoms also occur in affective disorder and coarse brain disease.) Gestures may be stiff, slow, and mannered; movements repetitive or incomplete; postures unnatural and maintained for long periods. Some patients make facial grimaces or speak with peculiar accents, others manifest echolalia (involuntary repetition of words spoken to the patient) or echopraxia (involuntary repetition of gestures made in the patient's presence), and still others become mute and immobile.

During the active phase of schizophrenia abnormal mental experiences, thought disorder, and catatonic symptoms are usually most prominent; during the chronic phase disturbances in emotional expression may be more evident. Although at times patients seem free of residual symptoms, some psychiatrists believe that a careful examination will usually reveal mild disturbances in thinking and emotional responsiveness. This is a moot point, which emphasizes again the difficulty in recognizing with confidence all symptoms of schizophrenia.

Classification of Schizophrenia

When Emil Kraepelin developed his concept of dementia praecox in the late nineteenth century, he included presentations earlier described as separate entities by Kahlbaum (catatonia), Hecker (hebephrenia), and Snell (paranoid psychosis or monomania). Despite their differing symptomatic features, Kraepelin grouped them, with dementia simplex, under a single heading because they shared a chronic deteriorating course, in contrast to the episodic, remitting course of manic-depressive illness. The classical subtypes of schizophrenia were thus distinguished by their predominant symptoms: in the catatonic form, psychomotor changes; in the hebephrenic, thought disorder and incongruity of mood; in the paranoid, delusions; and in the simple, loss of affective responsiveness and disturbances in will and drive.

At the onset of their illness, many patients present clinical pictures that fit these classical descriptions, but most eventually manifest such a variety of symptoms that assigning them to one or another group seems arbitrary. This fact has led to other attempts at distinguishing among schizophrenic illnesses for clues to etiology and outcome (for example, process versus reactive schizophrenia; schizophrenia versus schizophreniform states), but none has proven entirely satisfactory. We are almost certainly dealing with what Eugen Bleuler called the group of schizophrenias, and unless biological rather than psychological markers become available for some of them, it may not be possible to develop a classification for types of schizophrenia which is both reliable and clinically useful.

The fundamental feature of the symptoms of schizophrenia is that they are mental events in whose form it is impossible to perceive the cause and effect relationship that can be appreciated in normal psychological experience. Thus, we see perceptions without stimuli (hallucinations), beliefs without justification (delusions), thinking without logical connections (thought disorder), and emotions without issues and issues without emotions (the incongruous split of affective states from thought contents).

All the particular psychological experiences Schneider called first-rank symptoms belong here in a list of mental phenomena in which no glimmer of cause and effect relationship can be perceived. It is impossible, for example, to see such a connection in the experience of patients who hear voices comment on their actions or who believe that their thoughts are broadcast to the world. Symptoms and signs described by other psychiatrists as typically schizophrenic—Bleuler's thought disorder or Cameron's overinclusiveness—also share this lack of an obvious causal connection.

These experiences are called schizophrenic only when the patient shows no signs either of a primary change in affect or of coarse brain disease. When such evidence is present, the symptoms should always be ascribed to manic-depressive illness, delirium, or dementia. Schizophrenic symptoms are psychological events without explanations, and *without* is the operative word. It is clear that the ascription of a symptom as schizophrenic is an opinion based on exclusion rather than on positive evidence.

If a symptom can be called schizophrenic only if it is without explanation, then clearly the first responsibility of the diagnostician is to be sure that he cannot attribute it to another disorder. Since all of the abnormal mental experiences and disturbances of expression described above can be seen in manic-depressive illness, delirium, and dementia as well as in schizophrenia, those illnesses must be carefully excluded. Further, because disturbances in expression can occur in vulnerable people under stress, a consideration of the patient and his circumstances is required before it can confidently be stated that a symptom is inexplicable. An anxious and preoccupied person may, for example, have fragmented thinking; a naturally reserved individual can appear distant or cold; and a person of a different cultural heritage may express emotions in an unfamiliar manner. A detailed evaluation of the patient's personality and situation should be made before a symptom is said to be schizophrenic.

From this reasoning it is obvious that the diagnosis of schizophrenia betokens minimal understanding of the patient's illness. It indicates only that he suffers from a madness that is the residuum of having excluded other disorders. It is the oddest of psychiatric phenomena that this condition, essentially an admission of ignorance, is so often diagnosed, especially in situations that are unclear.

Psychiatrists would do well to make the diagnosis of schizophrenia as infrequently as possible. There is not only the danger of overlooking other conditions with different prognoses and treatments but also the risk that when a diagnosis resting on exclusion is used too often other things may be excluded too easily. The diagnostician's goal must be to find, if possible, a positive explanation for the patient's symptoms in other disorders or reactions. To do so requires a detailed history, repeated mental status examinations, and the readiness to consider a variety of formulations and to try a variety of treatments.

Possible Mechanisms and Etiologies of the Schizophrenic Syndrome: The Process of Validation

The definition of schizophrenia rests completely on a description of clinical features and course and on the exclusion of other conditions that share some of those features. We do not know enough about any pathological mechanisms or etiological agencies to make them part of the definition, nor can we recognize any characteristic clinical feature from which all the others can be derived. In using the disease concept we presume that schizophrenia is a clinical entity that may result from mechanisms and causes yet to be discovered. What gives us hope that such an opinion may be justified? As in manic-depressive illness, the evidence is indirect, but it points in the right direction.

First, the most characteristic clinical phenomena of schizophrenia and even aspects of its course can be seen as the symptomatic expressions of known brain disease. In their extensive review, Davison and Bagley list conditions, ranging from epilepsy to encephalitis and from Wilson's disease to cerebral trauma, that can produce a schizophrenia-like state in patients without genetic predisposition to schizophrenia[74]. Further, it is not brain damage in general that appears to be associated with symptomatic schizophrenia but lesions in the temporal lobes and diencephalon in particular.

Neuropathology has been reported for many years in patients with idiopathic schizophrenia, though the postmortem and pneumoencephalographic findings on which such observations rested were often criticized as artifacts. The development of more reliable diagnostic procedures for schizophrenia and the introduction of computerized axial tomography in the late 1970s have corrected many of these deficiencies. The work of Johnstone and colleagues in Britain and Weinberger and associates in the United States has demonstrated ventricular enlargement and sulcal widening in chronic schizophrenic patients, conditions that do not seem to be related to age, duration of illness, amount of neuroleptic medication, or length of hospitalization[75]. Although such findings may be nonspecific, since they are regular features of Alzheimer's disease and have also been seen in patients with manic-depressive illness, they suggest that reasoning from clinical syndrome to pathological disease entities is a legitimate approach to the explanation of schizophrenia.

Another body of work which suggests that the disease concept is appropriate for an understanding of schizophrenia is that derived from psychopharmacology. Here, as in manic-depressive illness, cerebral neurotransmitters are of great interest, and here, again, research was stimulated when a drug was observed to provoke a symptomatic condition closely resembling the spontaneously occurring disorder. Amphetamine use, especially if chronic, can induce a paranoid syndrome in individuals without genetic predisposition to schizophrenia—a paranoid syndrome in clear consciousness with delusions and hallucinations[76]. Even more striking, a dose-response relationship has been demonstrated, so there is a correlation between the dependent variable—a paranoid state—and the independent variable—the dose of dextroamphetamine[77]. The discoveries that amphetamine prolongs the effects of synaptically released dopamine and norepinephrine[78] and that drugs effective in the treatment of schizophrenia block dopamine receptors in the brain[11] have contributed to the proposal that the pathologic mechanisms involve biogenic amine neurotransmitters. Abnormalities in dopamine metabolism, dopamine receptors, or both, for example, may represent the pathological disease mechanisms responsible for a subgroup of schizophrenic illnesses[79].

As in manic-depressive illness, genetic factors appear to play a role in the cause of schizophrenia, though for both syndromes exactly what is inherited or how (that is, the mechanism by which genotype becomes phenotype) is unclear. Family studies have a long tradition in schizophrenia research and have repeatedly demonstrated an increasing risk for the disorder with increasing proximity of blood relationship to the proband. Further validation of the conclusions drawn from such work has come in the results of adoption studies. In Heston's pioneer research, for example, the psychiatric status of two groups of adoptees was compared: (1) the children of schizophrenic biological mothers raised in normal adoptive homes, and (2) the children of psychiatrically normal mothers raised in normal adoptive homes[80]. The rate of subsequent schizophrenia in the children of schizophrenic mothers was found to be significantly higher than that in the control group. A total national population sample of legally adopted adults in Denmark was studied by Kety and his colleagues, whose findings confirmed the importance of genetic factors in the etiology of schizophrenia[81]. Familial aggregation, though, is not the best evidence for a genetic disorder. That evidence, the Mendelian inheritance of schizophrenia, for example, must now be culled from family pedigrees. Even with such evidence, however, we must remember that this heterogeneous clinical entity can arise without known genetic predisposition; unidentified environmental factors may, therefore, play an important role in causation.

Schizophrenia and the Disease Concept

Our purpose in this chapter was to show how the disease concept could organize information about a condition that can as yet be defined only by its symptoms and course. If diagnosis must depend on such phenomena, then only the most reliably observed ones should be emphasized. When we understand the disorder better the most reliably recognized symptoms may in fact prove to be less important indicators of the condition; but until that time they are the best we have.

It was not our purpose to provide an encyclopedic review of research in schizophrenia but rather to show that such research tests and supports the presumption that schizophrenia rests on biological foundations. This work continues to validate the disease concept for the disorder.

As a category schizophrenia is disjunctive. It is hard to grasp even its conceptual essence beyond the fact of it as insanity. Yet conjunctive subcategories are emerging—for example, the symptomatic schizophrenia of amphetamine toxicity—and with them comes increasing clarity about mechanisms and etiologies in the entire group.

The organization of information through use of the disease concept does not end the argument over the nature of schizophrenia, but it supports the idea that the eventual explanation of the condition will derive from study of the brain's pathology.

The conditions discussed in chapters 7 and 8 do not exhaust all of the psychiatric disorders for which the disease concept may be suitable. Evidence is available that anorexia nervosa, phobic anxiety, and some forms of obsessional illness (all conditions without demonstrable neuropathology) may also be viewed in this way. It should be clear, however, that disease as a construct is not appropriate for all psychiatric issues. Disease should not be thought synonymous with symptoms such as pain or delusions, because they are the events to be explained by the construct. It should not be used to account for emotions such as anger or frustration, construed as the responses of a subject to stressful circumstances; nor should it be chosen to explain those personal vulnerabilities, like timidity or attention-seeking, that reflect constitutional and developmental variables; nor should the disease concept be immediately employed for behaviors such as delinquency or self-injury, the actions of individuals with particular intentions. Occasionally the term *disease* is employed for such issues, but its usage in this way should be regarded as metaphorical.

It is important to keep the traditional concept of disease separate from other models of human impairment. When we reason in terms of disease we seek cause in a disordered biology, and though this reasoning has been a successful convention, to adopt the disease concept as the only view of psychiatric problems would be to leave many patients poorly understood and poorly treated.

III

THE CONCEPT OF DIMENSIONS

9

Reasoning about Individual Differences as Dimensional Characteristics: The Assessment of Intelligence

Although the disease concept is a perspective that clearly illustrates the analysis of form in psychiatry, another perspective for this analysis is derived from the concept of individual differences. People vary in their psychological as well as physical characteristics. These differences can be viewed as a totality and termed personality or temperament, or they can be considered separately as attributes, traits, or aptitudes. Individual differences have provided thematic material for works of literature and for historical interpretations, and the attempt to explain them has a long history among the pseudosciences of astrology, physiognomy, and phrenology[82].

An important principle of modern psychiatry is that explanations of psychological differences should await the development of methods that can identify and measure them. This view springs most directly from the work of Francis Galton, the nineteenth-century English polymath: "An ordinary generalisation is nothing more than a muddle of vague memories of inexact observations. It is an easy vice to generalise. We want lists of facts, every one of which may be separately verified, valued and revalued, and the whole accurately summed"[83].

Galton brought this approach to studies of individual differences in perception, mental imagery, and word associations. In fact, as Fancher notes, it is from Galton that we have "the very *idea* that tests could be employed to measure psychological differences between people. . . . He thus elevated the scientific study of *individual differences* to the level of a major psychological specialty with important social implications"[84].

We are still struggling with the tasks that Galton began. Among the most important of them are disagreements over the definitions of the qualities under investigation, concerns about the sensitivity of the methods intended to discover these qualities, and the need to document both that the method chosen is reliable in its measurements (that is, that its results can be replicated) and that it is valid (that is, that it actually measures the feature it purports to assess).

In addition to these methodological problems there have been theoretical disputes among psychologists about what phenomena constitute proper objects of study (for example, disputes between Wundtian introspectionists and Watsonian behaviorists). Progress in the assessment of individual differences has even been affected by important political and philosophical questions concerning society's potential use and abuse of such data.

In this chapter we discuss the concept of individual differences in psychiatry and indicate those clinical problems for which it seems most appropriate. In that area in which its application has been the most successful—the assessment of intelligence—we will explain the relationship of the conclusions reached to the constructs and methods employed and indicate the difficulties in interpretation that arise out of the methods. In addition, we will exemplify some general principles needed to appreciate similar approaches to the assessment of other individual traits.

The Assessment of Intelligence

Many definitions of intelligence have been proposed—for example, mental efficiency, mental capacity, that quality required for scholastic success—but none has proven completely satisfactory. One reason definitions seem inadequate is that intelligence is not an object but a construct, useful in describing differences among people in their capacity to reason. It is easier to appreciate in action than to define. Many other features of the differences between individuals share this problem of definition.

In order to demonstrate intelligence, we can give people different cognitive tasks, each of which can be considered as an example, however impure, of intelligence in action, and score their achievement. From these scores inferences can be made about a subject's intelligence and how it compares with that of others, all without explicitly defining the term. If a sufficient number of tasks are studied, we can estimate intellectual capacity with increasing confidence.

This way of defining intelligence in practice is obviously not restricted to physicians or psychologists but is used in daily life. We estimate a person's intelligence by observing such things as his use of language, his judgment, his grasp of situations. Then, in light of our past experience with other individuals, we call him bright or dull and predict something of his future performance. Although their method is fundamentally the same, psychologists add scope to such judgments by requiring several different kinds of tasks before drawing their opinions; they also add accuracy to the observations by scoring the performance rather than relying on subjective impressions.

The first successful psychological tests of intelligence based on this reasoning were developed early in the century by Alfred Binet, in France[85]. The Minister of Public Instructions formed a committee intended to determine how mentally defective children could best be taught. Binet, a committee member, recognized that no decision of this sort could be made until some measure of the mental capacities of children had been found. He and his collaborator, Theodore Simon, used the approach of presenting cognitive tasks of progressive difficulty to groups of children ranging in age from three to twelve years. In this way they learned which tasks were successfully accomplished by most children at each year of age. With the knowledge of developmental stages and with these tasks as criteria, they could compare any given child's performance with that of others and assign him a "mental age," the age at which children usually performed as well as he did. It was a relatively simple step, first suggested by William Stern, to employ the ratio of mental age (MA) to chronological age (CA) multiplied by 100 (to eliminate decimals) as an intelligence quotient, or I.Q. Thus, if a child has an MA of 10 but a CA of 8, he has an I.Q. of 125.

This work satisfied the original need for a measure of intellectual capacity in children. How could it be applied to adults? Clearly the method of "mental age" would be unsatisfactory, since intellectual development progresses steadily with age only in the early years of life.

The use of the normal distribution curve in the selection of items made possible the development of tests suitable for adults. It was Galton who first demonstrated "that measurable intellectual characteristics tend to fall into *distributions* identical to those of inheritable physical traits. The Belgian statistician Adolph Quetelet (1796-1874) had already shown that measurements of physical characteristics such as height or weight fall into bell-shaped *normal distributions* if they are collected from many people. . . . Galton showed how normal distributions were also found in measures of *intellectual* ability"[86].

If test items are chosen so that the scores obtained are distributed in a normal curve, it is possible to scale the scores so that the mean score for a population is 100, corresponding to an average I.Q. of 100. The standard deviation (s.d.) then distributes the scores around the mean according to the principles of the normal curve. In this way any adult can be given an I.Q. score from his performance on a standard test. No ratio of mental to chronological age is used, but since psychologists have become familiar with the concept of an I.Q. of 100 as indicating average performance, similar numbers can be generated for adult tests. The most common tests, therefore, are standardized at a mean of 100, with only small differences in the standard deviation (Stanford-Binet s.d. = 16, Wechsler Adult Intelligence Scale s.d. = 15).

From results of studies with children and adults, intelligence appears to be a smoothly graded unimodal variable in the human population. Despite all efforts to get standardized norms, however, the distribution of scores is not perfectly symmetrical when whole populations are tested. There is a slightly greater number of individuals two standard deviations below the mean than two standard deviations above it, a point to which we shall return.

Throughout this century there have been many important attempts to define and measure intelligence. After Binet's work came the contributions of Spearman, Burt, Thurstone, Thomas, Piaget, Hebb, Cattell, and Wechsler. In their work on intelligence, as in the study of other individual differences, there are tensions between empirical observations and theoretical constructs, general and specific factors, static and developmental features, and the relationship of the characteristic in question to the organization of the nervous system[87].

In order to establish test scores (I.Q.'s) as a reasonable criterion for the psychological characteristic *intelligence,* the issues of reliability and validity had to be confronted. The reliability of standard tests is established, but their validity and the validity of the construct intelligence are still debated, especially when cross-cultural judgments are made from tests standardized on a restricted group.

An advantage of considering the construct intelligence as at least partially indicated by I.Q. is that it permits correlations with other variables to be drawn. One such relationship was the observation by Terman of personality features in very intelligent people. In contrast to a popular stereotype of the shy, introverted, or psychologically deranged genius, Terman and his colleagues demonstrated that intellectually gifted people tend much more often to be stable and personally effective[88].

With intelligence defined as an identifiable score, the problem of explanation emerges, and in this issue all the heat of the nature-nurture controversy is apparent. Again it was Galton who saw the matter clearly and who, in coining the phrase "nature and nurture," defined the terms of the debate:

> The phrase "nature and nurture" is a convenient jingle of words, for it separates under two distinct heads the innumerable elements of which personality is composed. Nature is all that a man brings with himself into the world; nurture is every influence that affects him after his birth. The distinction is clear: the one produces the infant such as it actually is, including its latent faculties of growth of body and mind; the other affords the environment amid which the growth takes place, by which natural tendencies may be strengthened or thwarted, or wholly new ones implanted[89].

That there is a hereditary component to intelligence seems established[90]. Among the strongest evidence for this are family, twin, and adoption studies that show I.Q. scores and biological relatedness to be positively correlated, so that monozygotic twins are most comparable in their intelligence levels.

(It is of particular interest that the statistical technique of correlation began with Francis Galton.)

Intelligence, like height, seems to have a polygenic heredity. Support for this view can be found in a phenomenon (yet another of Galton's observations) that is common to all smoothly graded polygenic traits: regression toward the mean from one generation to the next. Individuals who deviate markedly from the mean with respect to a certain characteristic will, on average, have children who move back toward the average for that characteristic. Because it is presumed that bright individuals provide an intellectually stimulating environment for their offspring, this result tends to refute the view that all intellectual capacity derives from its nurture. A tendency for scores to cluster around the mean in each generation explains why bright parents may have children not as bright as they—often a source of considerable distress in families of high intellectual achievement. Conversely, the children of dull-witted parents can be of normal or superior attainment, a fact that is usually a source of pride and happiness.

Environmental factors, particularly diseases, have been shown to have a detrimental effect on intelligence, whether that intelligence is developing (as in mental subnormality) or has been established (as in dementia). Positive environmental influences, especially social ones, are more difficult to establish, though findings such as Tuddenham's, which show significant increases in mean I.Q. scores in American soldiers from World War I to World War II[91], and Wheeler's, which demonstrate improvement in I.Q. scores in children in one region of Tennessee when social conditions improved[92], document their occurrence. Further, the work of Heber and Garber suggests that environmental intervention with infants and mothers can accelerate the intellectual development of children at risk for mental subnormality (though the long-term effects of that intervention are still unknown)[93]. Indeed, how human beings acquire intelligence and to what extent certain kinds of experience are essential to intellectual growth may be one of the most crucial problems in psychology.

If intelligence is defined by I.Q. tests developed for a particular population, the same test applied to other populations may show spurious distinctions between them. These issues of validity have yet to be resolved and are a source of argument between hereditarians and environmentalists. If our experience with height is a guide, it seems likely that inheritance sets some limit on cognitive ability, but that environmental circumstances, when adverse, can impose a much lower limit. In fact, as Butcher has pointed out, societies can be so different from one another that "what is given at birth" may assume almost any degree of relative importance for the eventual development of intelligence[94].

The nature-nurture problem seems to devolve into several arguments if the issue of the validity of intelligence tests is put aside. The proponents of most positions agree that it is useful to recognize that individuals are possessed of a general mental capacity that we can call intelligence, a capacity reflected in all of the diverse types of cognitive ability we know. The strict hereditarian would hold that differences in intelligence among individuals *and* among groups of individuals are the result of genetic differences. The strict environmentalist, on the other hand, would propose that although individuals may inherit all sorts of different specific mental capacities, the total genetic endowment is identical for each individual; thus, all differences in cognitive abilities for individuals *as well as* for groups are the result of different experiences. As in most such arguments, a middle ground fits much of the available data. This view holds that individuals inherit different mental capacities and differ in their total genetic endowment for intelligence. On the other hand, large human groups such as nations or races do not differ significantly in their genetic pools for intellectual capacity. All intergroup differences in cognitive ability are the result of those environmental differences and life experiences that distinguish one group from another. Further, whatever proportion of variance in intelligence we ascribe to heredity, for practical purposes society can act and plan as though environmental influences are crucial.

Although intelligence tests may be abused to stigmatize individuals or to deprive them of opportunity, our evaluative judgments would be more difficult without them. To rely solely on personal and perhaps idiosyncratic judgments of intelligence is to risk both underestimating the capacities of individuals stigmatized in other ways (for example, by race, poverty, deformity) and denying to those with intellectual deficits the assistance and opportunities provided by a compassionate society.

Intelligence testing, however controversial, has been successful as long as its limits have been recognized. Its great accomplishment in predicting scholastic performance was perhaps the major stimulus for the development of other psychological tests, which attempt to assess other individual differences. Although not originally designed to aid psychiatrists in dealing with patients, this work has furthered our understanding of several forms of mental disorder and is central to the topic of mental subnormality.

10

Mental Subnormality & the Problem of Categorical Distinctions Derived from Dimensional Traits

The defining feature of mental subnormality is a lifelong deficit in intellectual capacity. For centuries, this particular deficit has distinguished the subnormal from others with mental difficulties. As John Locke observed: "Madmen put wrong ideas together, and so make wrong propositions, but argue and reason right from them; but idiots make very few or no propositions, and reason scarce at all"[95]. In recent years, in various classifications, additional characteristics have been proposed and debated (for example, whether or not social incompetence, poor adaptive behavior, or persistent educational failure should be included), but all psychiatrists agree that the term *mental subnormality* is meaningless without defective intelligence.

It is helpful here to emphasize a distinction between the concept of impairment and the concept of disability caused by that impairment. One may, for example, have an impairment in hematopoiesis (anemia) with or without experiencing any disability (for example, weakness). So, too, one may have an impairment in intelligence (mental subnormality) with or without experiencing any disability (for example, occupational failure). It is essential to recognize mental subnormality in individuals disabled by it and, despite the risk of stigmatization, such recognition may be desirable even in people without current problems, so impairments may be remedied, vulnerabilities understood, and future disabilities avoided.

We prefer the term *mental subnormality* to what is perhaps a more traditional expression, *mental retardation. Retardation* is an appropriate term for those individuals who are both slow to acquire intellectual capacity and limited in their attainment, but there are others who do not give any early evidence of slow development, being deficient only in the capacity eventually reached. Subnormality adequately describes both groups.

Mental subnormality was recognized long before intelligence scores or I.Q. tests were developed, but with such scores it is possible to employ a quantitative definition of the term. A common practice is to restrict the class of mentally subnormal individuals to those who fall two standard deviations below the mean I.Q. for the population. Thus, depending on whether the Stanford-Binet or the Wechsler Adult Intelligence Scale is used, anyone with an I.Q. below 68 or 70 would be classified as subnormal.

This technique of classification by test score is helpful for some, but not all, clinical purposes. As we have described it and as the I.Q. scores are designed to reflect it, intelligence is a smoothly graded dimensional variable with no discontinuities. It is a trait recognizable to a greater or lesser degree in everyone. Where to say normality begins or ends is arbitrary, then, even though it is not difficult to recognize an extremely impaired individual.

How, for example, should a person with an I.Q. of 75 be viewed? Does he fall outside the category of the impaired because he is only one and one-half standard deviations below the mean? And since a variation of eight points on repeat testing is not unusual, would a second test score of 67 then make him impaired? Obviously not. The cutoff of two standard deviations below the mean has been chosen recognizing its arbitrariness, with the expectation that disabilities due to intellectual deficit will be very common in individuals below that point, whereas disabilities attributed to intellectual deficit will be increasingly less common above it. We have drawn a distinction at a convenient mathematical point on an unbroken curve, a distinction that identifies a group of people that clinical experience has shown often have trouble because of the impairment represented by their position on such a curve.

The strengths and weaknesses of this approach, in which seemingly arbitrary decisions parcel out into categories individuals who are at the extreme ends of a smoothly graded dimensional characteristic, will be considered again for other traits, but it is a method most easily demonstrated with the mentally subnormal. We must remember, however, that despite its common use and proven utility, it is only a convention and does not replace the need for evaluating patients to discover the sources of their difficulties. It is still the responsibility of psychiatrists to recognize individuals whose troubles derive in part from a lack of the intellectual power required to be successful in a given circumstance, even among those whose I.Q. scores do not fall below the arbitrary two-standard-deviations criterion, just as it is our responsibility to recognize the abilities, intellectual and otherwise, of those whose scores do.

Further subclassification into mild (I.Q. 69-55), moderate (54-40), severe (39-25), and profound (24 and below) subnormality is also possible by taking single standard deviation units to form the groups. Again, these are arbitrary divisions, but they are intended to imply some distinctions in degree of deficit which may have helpful prognostic associations. For example, although they need guidance in periods of distress, the mildly subnormal can acquire many basic academic skills and are capable of social and vocational functioning that brings a variable degree of self-support, including complete independence. Many such people are indistinguishable from the rest of the community and have never been recognized as subnormal[96]. The moderately subnormal are trainable in social and vocational skills but will always need direction and sheltering, as their capacities do not reach beyond about the second-grade level. The severely disabled do not profit much from training, but can develop self-protective skills and habits of cleanliness, whereas the profoundly subnormal need nursing care, being only minimally able to look after themselves.

Although for purposes of definition we have focused on the smoothly graded character of intelligence in the population, we mentioned earlier that the I.Q. curve is not perfectly symmetrical. There are more individuals two standard deviations below the mean than there are two standard deviations above it. This observation can be made whenever a total population sample is drawn, if care is taken not to miss any individual, including those in institutions.

E. O. Lewis pointed out in his survey of an English county that this asymmetry is produced mainly by finding a larger number of individuals among the more severely defective (below I.Q. 50) than would be expected from a perfect Gaussian curve (fig. 3)[97].

The following table shows the percentages that Lewis found in various I.Q. categories and compares them with the percentages predicted from a normal distribution:

	0-20 I.Q.	*20-50 I.Q.*	*50-70 I.Q.*	*Total*
Predicted	0.00%	0.04%	2.23%	2.27%
Discovered	0.06%	0.24%	2.26%	2.56%

The percentage of people found in the highest I.Q. category is essentially what would be expected from a normal distribution, but there are six times as many people as would be expected in the lower categories. Lewis could explain these findings only after examining the individuals, whereupon he observed that two different groups are found among the intellectually subnormal.

One group, people whom he called subculturally or physiologically subnormal, is made up of individuals who are the counterparts of the intellectually gifted in the population. They have apparently intact nervous systems, are mostly mildly subnormal (clustering in the 50-70 I.Q. range), and are the expected contributions to the lower end of a normal distribution. They have parents who are on the low side of the mean for I.Q., and they are more heavily represented among socially deprived families. A combination of nature

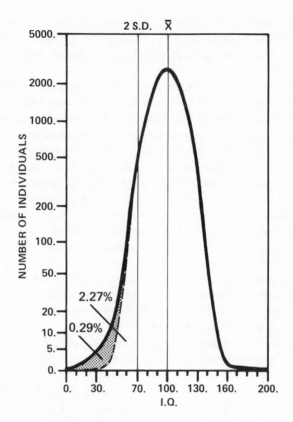

FIGURE 3 Theoretical distribution of intelligence test scores in a total population ($\bar{x}$ = mean, S.D. = Standard Deviation). Adapted from L. S. Penrose, *The Biology of Mental Defect* (London: Sidgwick and Jackson, 1963).

and nurture seems to have led to their deficits, and they represent the majority (75-80 percent) of the mentally subnormal.

The other group consists of individuals who were brain damaged during conception, gestation, or birth. Lewis called these individuals the pathologically subnormal, and though they are the minority (no more than 25 percent of the subnormal population), most have I.Q.'s below 50. Their brain defects are usually recognizable and produce many neurological abnormalities as well as intellectual deficits. Their parents are distributed equally around the mean for I.Q., and they are not overrepresented among the socially deprived.

It is the second group that gives the asymmetrical character to the I.Q. curve. In fact, the asymmetry of the I.Q. curve is best understood as a form of bimodality on this dimension of human variability—intelligence. At the lower end there is a small mode consisting mostly of brain-damaged individuals and a small number of apparently undamaged ones. As the dimension is ascended, the brain-damaged drop out and the major mode of the intelligence capacities of the undamaged appears, peaks at I.Q. 100, and comes down to a normal tail at the high end.

We have, in fact, one trait, but within the population displaying that trait there are two groups of people producing what would be a clear bimodal distribution if the number in the pathologically subnormal group were greater. With so few individuals surviving brain injuries until they can be tested, however, they are reflected only as an asymmetry in the lower tail of the curve. Issues of bimodality in trait distributions will be recognized in other psychiatric disorders, but they are most clearly demonstrated in the mentally subnormal.

Although it is not our purpose to examine in detail the specific causes of pathological subnormality, there are some representative examples that make useful points for psychiatrists. In this group are found all kinds of brain disease, particularly those related to infections, malformations, trauma, asphyxia, and endocrine disorders during development. These patients suffer from neurological symptoms that vary with the nature and location of their pathology, including epilepsy, motor-sensory impairments, perceptual disorders, and abnormalities of growth and body structure. Their disabilities derive from more than just their intellectual impairment. They present with recognizable clinical syndromes for which the disease concept is appropriate. The major issue for the future with regard to this group of conditions causing subnormality is how to improve efforts at preventing these relatively well-described pathological states and etiological agencies.

Two particular forms of biological pathology that can provoke mental subnormality need emphasis because they demonstrate important principles. The first is genetic disorder. In the population of the pathologically subnormal, single-gene disorders are common, and the afflicted are usually homozygous for a recessive gene. Dominant-gene disorders are seldom found among the mentally subnormal because, if they appear as mutations, they are quickly eliminated from the genetic pool owing to the reduced fertility of the mentally subnormal. Recessive genes that manifest their symptoms only when seen in the homozygotic state are preserved longer in the genetic pool because heterozygotes are clinically unaffected.

A classical example of such a recessive condition is phenylketonuria. In this disorder, the homozygotic individual is deficient in phenylalanine hydroxylase, an enzyme critical to the formation of tyrosine and thus to several important neurotransmitters. Without the enzyme, phenylalanine accumulates because it cannot be metabolized. These patients show high levels of phenylalanine in their blood and cerebrospinal fluid and spill the metabolic products of that amino acid in their urine. They can be protected from developing the clinical manifestations of the disease (which include small stature, convulsions, and eczema in addition to severe mental subnormality) if they maintain a diet low in phenylalanine during their early years.

This condition exemplifies many of the issues raised by recessive genetic disorders. First, such disorders produce a very severe mental subnormality if no treatment is found. Second, a biochemical abnormality can often be recognized and attributed directly to some enzyme lack. Third, the conditions are more common in consanguineous matings, because individuals who share something of a common genetic pool are more likely to share a rare gene arising from a common ancestor than are unrelated individuals. Fourth, the search for carriers of the recessive gene (heterozygotes) has great importance for genetic counseling. In phenylketonuria it is possible to identify such heterozygotes because, with only one normal gene for the enzyme and thus a smaller amount of it, they are slower than normal in metabolizing phenylalanine (although not so slow as to be injured by it). Finally, for phenylketonuria and similar disorders, there is a need to learn how the biochemical abnormalities affect the developing brain so that better modes of protection can be found.

The group of pathologically subnormal individuals with gene disorders should be distinguished from the group with abnormalities in the number or structure of their chromosomes. Chromosomal abnormalities can be produced in either gametogenesis or embryogenesis and can affect either all or some of the cells in the body (mosaicism). The development of standard cytological techniques for the identification and typing of chromosomes has occurred only in the last two decades, but already hundreds of chromosomal disorders have been described. The most common of these to produce severe mental subnormality is Down's syndrome (trisomy 21). Here, the generalized chromosomal abnormality affects development in the brain, impairing intelligence, just as it affects other parts of the body, causing defects in stature, appearance, dentition, and the functioning of internal organs. Most of the syndromes of mental subnormality associated with chromosomal anomalies have been described as resulting from abnormalities of autosomes, and, although abnormality in the number of sex chromosomes can produce clear physical stigmata (as in Turner's syndrome and Klinefelter's syndrome), it seems to produce, on the whole, less intellectual impairment than does autosomal abnormality. Recently, a morphological abnormality on the X chromosome has been described, an abnormality that may account for a large number of mild-to-moderately subnormal males (and perhaps also some females) who might have been thought to form part of the subculturally subnormal population[98].

To better understand the intellectual impairment of pathologically subnormal individuals, we must recognize that they are qualitatively defective organisms. These patients are injured, and their injury appears not only in lessened ability but also in imperfect and unequal development of their capacities. The natural schedules of development which lead to a balance of capacities are as vulnerable to brain injury as are the skills themselves. As a result, whereas the concept of reduced mental age is a reasonable description for the impairment in the physiologically subnormal individual, because intellectually he does resemble a normal person of younger chronological age, the concept is inadequate for the psychology of the pathologically subnormal person, because he poorly resembles a normal child of comparable mental age[99].

For the pathologically subnormal, developmental milestones are often passed much more slowly and usually less successfully, with frequent lapses in control once achieved. Speech, for example, often appears late and in some individuals breaks down temporarily under emotional stress. It will be apparent long before school that the child is impaired in many functions; he has difficulty in reasoning and is not just slow to learn. Many of these children appear apathetic and uninterested in the world around them, but others may show intense concern for and even exaggerated skills in one endeavor to the detriment of others. Thus, hoarding of objects, calculation of dates, and rigidities of schedule may endanger the relationships such people have with others. It is the combination of deficits and exaggerations in mental life that gives these individuals a lack of harmony, or mental disequilibrium, analogous to their motor-sensory disequilibrium from brain injury, and in this way they are often quite different from normal children of comparable mental age.

Despite the cognitive and physical impairments attendant upon pathological mental subnormality, many of these individuals can lead lives of dignity and fulfillment. Not to recognize their particular vulnerabilities, however, would be to overlook potentials for psychiatric disorder, including the illnesses mentioned in chapters 5, 7, and 8. The mentally subnormal (and particularly the brain-damaged among them) seem especially prone to such disorders. Data from the Camberwell Study, for example, suggest that the prevalence of schizophrenia is greater among the mentally subnormal than among the rest of the population[100]. Individuals with Down's syndrome seem particularly at risk to develop a dementing illness with the neuropathological changes of Alzheimer's disease[101]. Because dementia occurs among the mentally subnormal, it is useful to distinguish the two concepts; thus, we would diagnose dementia, rather than subnormality, to describe a deterioration in intellectual capacity from previously established levels, whatever those levels were and whenever (including the developmental period) the deterioration began.

In the mildly subnormal individual, delirium, dementia, manic-depressive illness, and schizophrenia can all be diagnosed by their usual clinical criteria, though as Reid[102] and others have pointed out, the verbal skills of people with I.Q.'s below 45 or 50 are often insufficient to permit recognition of characteristic abnormal mental experiences, so the diagnosis must often rest on changes in behavior and emotional expression (for example, periodic alterations in socialization, activity level, and sleep could suggest manic-depressive illness). For similar reasons, the treatments for these disorders need especially careful monitoring in subnormal patients, who will be able to contribute less than other people to the assessment of their progress. The mentally subnormal with mental illnesses have a double burden to bear and, unfortunately, are often doubly stigmatized.

Subculturally or physiologically subnormal individuals differ from the rest of the population only in their intellectual capacity. This difference is quantitative and seldom more than moderate in degree. As organisms, they are relatively deficient in a general ability in the same way that other people can be relatively deficient in physical strength, coordination, or endurance. Their deficit is seldom evident until they face tasks, such as school or employment, that demand a certain level of reasoning and judgment for satisfactory results.

Thus, as young children, it is often only when school begins that their relative lack of intelligence is recognized. Their earlier developmental milestones, such as talking, walking, and toilet training, are usually attained at suitable ages, and, although a sharp appraisal might have discovered difficulties, the range of normal for infants is so great and the requirements for successful transit through this stage so few that a diagnosis is seldom made. Rather, the difficulty is in learning abstract concepts. Reading, computation, and reasoning from evidence come slowly and the eventual level obtained is low.

In part, a low level of achievement for these individuals may be the result of learning under disadvantageous conditions. As Bortner and Birch have noted, there is an important distinction to be made between an individual's cognitive performance (how he does in particular circumstances) and his cognitive capacity (the ability and skills he actually possesses and could manifest in appropriate conditions)[103]. Intensified instruction is helpful, and a great need exists for teachers who appreciate the importance of even small gains with respect to future opportunities for these people.

Later in life the vulnerabilities of the mildly subnormal may again be submerged, particularly if the person is in a settled routine of interaction and occupation, such as that of a housewife with a supportive family or a laborer with simple daily tasks. Only with the disruption of such situations (the death of a spouse or the closing of an industry) do the relative impairments of these people again become apparent as disabilities. It is, therefore, in the periods of life marked by the need for analysis, learning, and change that such individuals demonstrate their vulnerabilities and are potentially at risk for emotional distress. This latter aspect of the psychiatry of mental subnormality is often underemphasized, yet, as subject/agents with intentions and aims, mentally subnormal individuals experience difficulties that must be recognized if they are to be resolved. These individuals are deficient in one of the most crucial tools by which a person can construe, interpret, and plan. They are thus vulnerable to feelings of discouragement and to emotional expressions of anxiety, depression, and frustration if what they intend is thwarted by a combination of circumstances and their own inability to formulate a success-ful plan of action. Anxiety and frustration then act to reduce still further, albeit temporarily, their cognitive efficiency. A downward spiral of failure, depression, further failure, and intense emotional reaction is often discernible as one listens to the patient's worries and hears how they relate to his aims and what ideas he has had to resolve them. The confusion of purposes, the par-ticulars of difficulty (inability to balance a checkbook, deal with a teacher, avoid exploitation, etc.), and the sense of being frightened, overwhelmed by circumstances, paralyzed by indecision, and depressingly isolated—these characteristic problems are elicited in a sympathetic interview and can be understood as manifestations of despair. Intellectual subnormality made the patient vulnerable to this reaction, but circumstances provoked it.

Summary

We have discussed mental subnormality at some length in order to illustrate several points about conditions that can be understood as disturbances along dimensions of human variation. First, though there is argument over the construct intelligence, the idea that individuals vary along this dimension can easily be appreciated in the clinic. Second, we can identify çategories of individuals from within the dimension, but only by arbitrary demarcations along the continuum. Third, someone's position on the dimension can depend on many factors. Brain disease is but one factor, though when it occurs it is usually productive of a stereotyped clinical syndrome that includes phenomena other than intellectual deficits. Finally, this example from intelligence demon-strates that deviation along a dimension of variation can itself place an in-dividual at risk for emotional distress when he faces particular circumstances.

11

The Assessment of Traits Other Than Intelligence & the Concept of Personality Disorder

We have argued that the disease concept, with its distinct categories resting on the recognition of symptom clusters, pathological entities, and etiological agencies, is not the only explanatory perspective for psychopathology. We can construe a dimension of variation in psychological characteristics and see impairment in people who deviate to an extreme along that dimension. Intelligence is just such a construal, and, at least among individuals who rest on the low side of the dimension, a number of particular and consistent problems can be found and explained by their position on that dimension. Our purpose now is to demonstrate that the essential premise of dimensions of variation can illuminate other clinical issues.

Since the ancient Greeks, people have noted constellations of psychological characteristics among their fellows. The descriptions of these personality types, such as the sanguine and the choleric, are so apt that we instantly recognize them today, even though they are presented in languages and concepts (such as the humoral theory) long dead. People who are very neat may well also be perfectionistic, conscientious, and self-doubting (today called the compulsive personality type), while those who are self-dramatizing also tend to be emotionally labile and egocentric (the hysterical or histrionic personality type)[104]. Types are ideals, so individuals may have prominent attributes of several types, and a group said to be representative of a certain type will include examples that merge with the normal population.

There are several problems with typological reasoning. First, it proposes categories that are usually awkwardly disjunctive. We sense a central concept but are hard put to agree on its boundaries. Thus, by the term *hysterical personality* we mean a combination of features that includes self-dramatization, emotional lability, and egocentricity in a variety of patterns. The essence of the type is, however, elusive. The third edition of the *Diagnostic and Statistical*

Manual of Mental Disorders (*DSM-III*), the official classification of the American Psychiatric Association, has changed the term from *hysterical* to *histrionic* in order to clarify the category[105]. Jaspers, in a similar attempt to find the central feature of the type, proposed that such individuals "crave to appear . . . as more than they are" [106].

Next, types are poorly tied to phenomena beyond themselves. They are not categories like diseases, linked to pathological mechanisms and etiological agencies that can be detected by laboratory examinations. For this reason, the thoughtless use of personality types may seem little more than unprofessional name-calling.

This is just another way of saying that typologies are difficult to validate. This difficulty accounts for the multiplicity of distinct types of personality that have been described. Each type is often vividly portrayed by its author, who may even propose operational criteria for its recognition. But operationalism is not validation. Validation of types requires observations that clearly discriminate one type from another or observations, based on different methods, that provide convergent evidence for the existence of the type.

Yet the combination of a vulnerable individual and stressful circumstances is central to reasoning about psychiatric disorder from the perspective of individual differences. Although there are circumstances that everyone finds stressful—for example, prolonged combat, natural disaster, the death of a loved one—psychiatrists do not usually see patients under the provocation of such events. Much more often, psychiatrists find that people troubled by their situations have some particular vulnerability that renders them liable to emotional distress in specific circumstances, even though others would not be as upset by such events. For example, a mentally subnormal person is distressed by demands on his powers of abstract thinking that someone of normal intelligence would master without difficulty; a very dependent person becomes upset and suicidal at the end of a relationship whose termination might have gladdened most people; an extremely fussy person is angered and frustrated when dealing with a subordinate whose performance most supervisors would find adequate. Ernst Kretschmer termed the events that elicit a characteristic response from a particular vulnerability *key experiences* because individuality and situation fit together like a lock and key to release an emotional reaction[107].

Individual vulnerabilities can lie in dimensional psychological characteristics of personality other than intelligence. *Personality* describes an individual's abiding and distinctive traits, his tendencies to react to circumstances in a particular fashion. When the term *personality* is used in this way it is clear that we are implicitly comparing one individual with others and that the constituent traits of a personality can be considered as dimensions along which people vary in much the same way as they vary in other characteristics, such as height or intelligence. Just as people are taller or shorter, brighter or duller,

so, too, they are more or less optimistic or pessimistic, dependent or independent, conscientious or carefree, suspicious or trusting. This perspective
implies that there are dimensional traits along which people vary rather than
types into which they are pigeonholed.

A number of points relate to this concept. Our decisions about particular
traits rest on observations and measurements that must ultimately confront
the issues of reliability and validity. These issues may be satisfied in the future,
but as yet there are only a few traits for which we have commonly used
measures of proven reliability and validity as for intelligence.

It is also apparent that any given individual can be described by a number
of different traits, including his intelligence, and that for each one he has a
position along a dimension of variation. The point at which normal is divided
from abnormal on these dimensions may seem arbitrary and be difficult to
judge. When, for example, does normally conscientious behavior become
obsessionally perfectionistic? Distinctions are clear enough at the extremes,
but observers may differ on the precise point at which they diagnose deviation,
just as they may disagree about whom they call dull or bright on the intelligence
dimension. In clinical practice, the criterion for what can usefully be considered abnormal is the recognition that a patient is so deviant in respect of
one or more traits that he is thereby rendered vulnerable, in the sense that
he or others suffer because he is so dependent, irritable, or self-dramatizing.

Since traits describe how a person tends to respond to certain situations,
the concept of personality also implies circumstance. Thus, for example, the
term *paranoid personality* implies an individual who responds with suspiciousness and feelings of persecution to settings so minimally threatening that they
seldom provoke such responses in others. Despite a persistent vulnerability of
personality, however, these attitudes will disappear when that person is in a
setting he believes to be free from threat.

The clinical assessment of personality rests on the patient's self-description,
the reports of others about him, and psychiatrists' interactions with him. To
the extent that these techniques vary in form and content they will vary in
reliability, and sometimes there is little agreement about global personality
diagnoses (though there is more for ratings of individual traits) even when a
standardized method is used[108]. Still, clinical assessment is an ongoing and
adaptable process, and methods of acceptable reliability (for example, the
Standardized Assessment of Personality [109]) are in increasing use.

Questionnaires such as the Minnesota Multiphasic Personality Inventory
have also been used to assess traits, but they should not replace assessment
based on the history and on repeated interviews. These tests ask a series of
specific questions and compare a given patient's responses with those of
others previously studied. The individual clinician is limited to judging a
personality from his own experience. Personality tests make a standardized
comparison with much larger groups. This advantage, however, must be

offset by the fact that test scores are often greatly influenced by the patient's emotional state at the time of testing; rather than reveal abiding traits of personality, therefore, tests may actually reflect temporary states of mind, such as depression, anger, or anxiety[110]. Personality tests are not the psychiatric equivalent of x-rays, and though they can complement a detailed history and repeated observations of a patient, they are no substitute for them.

As in the concept of intelligence, progress in the definition and assessment of personality traits has occurred despite theoretical disputes and methodological problems. Can traits be assessed by questionnaire or only be observed in action? Are the various techniques reliable and valid? In addition to issues such as these, psychologists face a major problem because there are thousands of words in English that are appropriate as trait names[111]. Which are clinically relevant? One solution to these questions came from the statistical techniques whose development began with Galton. Factor analysis provides a means whereby many separate measurements can be correlated and from them traits derived that more parsimoniously account for variations observed. The technique of factor analysis has been used productively by many workers, but by none more than Hans Eysenck and his associates.

Eysenck's group began with psychiatrists' ratings of thirty-nine personality traits in 700 neurotic military men [112]. A factorial study of the intercorrelations of these traits revealed two major dimensions of variation: neuroticism-stability and introversion-extraversion, personality dimensions that had previously been described and that have subsequently been replicated in other populations.

The dimensions of neuroticism-stability and introversion-extraversion are important. Like the dimension of intelligence, they can be identified throughout the population and thus assessed in both normal individuals and patients by utilizing test instruments (such as the Eysenck Personality Inventory) of acceptable reliability. These two traits have been shown to have clinical relevance in many studies, starting with Eysenck's first, in which he demonstrated that patients high on neuroticism and high on introversion tended to have "dysthymic" diagnoses (anxiety, reactive depression, obsessions) whereas those high on neuroticism and high on extraversion received hysterical and psychopathic diagnoses [113].

Yet the validation of traits such as introversion-extraversion and neuroticism-stability is problematic. We do not have an ultimate criterion, such as the demonstration of a disorder in a bodily part, to validate them. The fundamental question for such issues is, What is the nature of personality dimensions? The question is answered by proposing that the construct of traits underlies characteristic differences in test performance[114]. The validation of a trait construct depends on two kinds of evidence: discriminatory and convergent.

We discriminate when we demonstrate that the measures of the trait are specific for that trait and not for others. This has been shown for introversion-extraversion and for neuroticism-stability. They are unrelated and form two distinct dimensions of personality. It is therefore possible to view individuals as varying in warmth, gregariousness, assertiveness, and excitement seeking (the extraversion-introversion dimension) and in anxiety-proneness, hostility, self-consciousness, and vulnerability to depression (the neuroticism-stability dimension).

Discrimination, however, is not convergent evidence. A major validation for these constructs is that Eysenck's measures have been confirmed in both strength and character by measures derived from other methods. Thus, despite many theoretical and technical differences in the measures developed by Eysenck, Cattell, and Guilford, all three of these investigators produced empirical results that converge in revealing these two basic dimensions of personality. Eysenck's *neuroticism* correlates with Cattell's *anxiety* and Guilford's *emotional health*; Eysenck's *extraversion* with Cattell's *exvia* and Guilford's *social activity* [115].

Another piece of convergent evidence validating these constructs as enduring traits is the demonstration that they actually endure. In fact, the scores an individual achieves at one time on these measures predict the scores he will achieve at some later time. Costa and McCrae give evidence in the form of retest correlations of 0.73 in the Guilford characteristics over twelve-year intervals in adults. Such high correlations are evidence of both the stability of these measures and the validity of the enduring trait construct itself[115].

Dimensions have proven easier to replicate and to validate than have typologies. They lead us to appreciate the typologies in a new way. It is, as Eysenck has shown, those individuals who deviate to the extremes on his dimensions who suffer or cause others to suffer in many circumstances. In addition, such ancient types as the choleric and the sanguine can be seen as categories derived from a parceling of individuals who are related across dimensions of human variation.

In recent years there has been a debate among psychologists about whether personality is best accounted for by trait theory, which posits relatively stable characteristics that have a causal role in behavior and depend on factors "inside" the person, or by social learning theory, which seeks to account for behavioral tendencies through concepts like operant conditioning and factors "outside" the person. As Endler and Magnusson set the question: "Is behavior consistent across situations, or is it situation-specific?" [116]. As in the nature-nurture debate over intelligence, the best answer seems to be both.

Despite the crucial role the environment plays in the manifestation of personality, to some important degree the potential for certain reactions is present from birth. Support for that view comes from studies demonstrating differences in autonomic reactivity and behavior in neonates[117] and from genetic research that suggests a strong hereditary component to personality in monozygotic twins raised apart[118]. As with intelligence, however, we cannot assume that what seems "given" prior to life experience cannot be changed by that experience. In every person both constitution and circumstance can be assessed for their relative contributions to an individual's vulnerability to distress.

The advantages that accrue from the trait approach to personality and from the identification of dimensions such as introversion-extraversion and neuroticism-stability are identical to those found in the identification of the dimension intelligence: This perspective provides a powerful and valid conceptual framework for understanding individual vulnerabilities without becoming lost in the endlessness of individuals themselves. Much is explained, though much remains unexplained[119].

12

Emotions &
Their Relationship to
Life Events &
Personality Traits

The concept of personality traits discussed in the last chapter implies that deviation along any of a number of dimensional characteristics renders the individual vulnerable to respond with distress to particular life circumstances. In this chapter we elaborate on this concept by focusing on the nature of particular emotional responses and on their links to traits.

Whereas traits indicate potential, it is life circumstances that provoke emotional responses. Trait-related potentials and situational provocations can vary independently, acting as kinds of vector forces to evoke a response. Thus, a person who is very vulnerable with respect to a certain trait may need little stress to provoke a degree of dysphoric emotional response that would occur only with extreme stress in a less vulnerable individual.

In chapter 11 we indicated some of the complexity of the issue of traits. The matter of life events may be even more complicated, as it includes not only obvious disasters like bereavement or injury but also situations so subtle and symbol laden that their relationship to the emotional response is not at first evident.

Certain situations are conducive to provoking the emotional responses of anxiety or sadness in almost anyone[120], but in vulnerable people less extreme circumstances elicit these same responses, which might then be called neurotic because they are so much more readily evoked and because their degree and duration seem disproportionate to the situation.

This approach to emotional responses is different from that of the disease concept, in which the primary focus is on mental events as derangements of the object/organism. We employ the category *disease* with its logical development from clinical entity to etiological agency, in order to utilize current biological knowledge and so to define treatment and to indicate directions for research. The success of this method should not, however, make us overlook the limitations of its applicability. There are many clinical situations in which the patient's difficulty is characterized, not by a processlike disruption of mental state, but rather by the distressing excess of some commonly felt emotion, by a quantitative rather than a qualitative abnormality. The patient and his family complain, for example, that he is more often anxious than others or that he is discouraged, demoralized, or uncertain more frequently than seems warranted.

Here, the disease method is not adequate and in fact misleads if employed. What is most apparent is not a stereotyped set of symptoms with a relentless course indicative of some class of disorder but a troubled person expressing natural feelings and complaining that they are excessive and distressing. How are we to appreciate these issues and how can we devise an interpretative schema that accomplishes as much for the troubled person as the concept of disease does for the impaired?

This is the area of psychiatry in which the method of understanding shifts from the determinism of biology to the appreciation of meaning in human behavior. We turn from the language of object/organisms (disease, symptoms, natural history, mechanism, cause) to a language of subject/agents (feelings, intentions, assessments, actions, responses). We attempt to understand these patients as people with intelligible plans and comprehensible responses derived from personal characteristics and life circumstances. We expect to find meaning in the choices such patients make and in the emotions they express, and we conceive of treatment in terms of persuasion, insight, and alternative rather than repair or replacement.

It is the point of this book that, although no psychiatry is complete without an appreciation of the patient as both subject/agent and object/organism, the conceptual distinctions between these views of the patient should not be blurred, no matter how intermingled their expressions become on a clinical level. In this blurring lies one of the greatest sources of confusion in psychiatry. Thus, even the word *neurosis,* the term most often used for the conditions under discussion, is directly linked to *nervous* and *nerves,* a link that emphasizes elements of the organism in the very situation in which they are probably least pertinent.

Few words in psychiatry are as troublesome as *neurosis,* which presents problems in concept and usage. Sometimes *neurosis* is used to imply a discrete entity, separate from *psychosis* but also separate from normal mental life in the way that a disease state is thought qualitatively distinct from normal. At other times *neurosis* is used to describe part of a theoretical continuum of mental life that extends from normal through the mildly abnormal (neurotic) to the severely abnormal (psychotic). This muddle can be resolved by considering affective disorder and schizophrenia as clinical disease entities whose pathologies and etiologies remain to be discovered. Neuroses, on the other hand, are examples of emotional reactions to life situations, are named by the most prominent response in what is usually a mix of several, and find their abnormality only in quantitative features such as the frequency, duration, or intensity of the reaction. It might thus be advisable to avoid the use of the noun *neurosis* with its preconceptions of entity, perhaps retaining the adjective *neurotic* as a shorthand expression for emotional responses that seem quantitatively excessive. Here we are considering not disease entities but rather modes of emotional expression that can be interpreted and explained in terms of potential, provocation, and response. Personalities are the potentials, life circumstances are the provocations, and neurotic symptoms are the responses.

To exemplify this approach we will consider the emotional state of anxiety, a universal experience in situations of threat and uncertainty. That anxiety is not a completely destructive and inappropriate emotion is shown by the classical Yerkes-Dodson law—the "inverted U" relationship between arousal and performance skills. This relationship indicates that for any given task the presence of some anxiety, with its accompanying arousal and attentiveness, improves performance, but as anxiety increases the skillfulness of the performance peaks and then rapidly declines. The difficulty of the task determines the turning point. In easy tasks anxiety improves skill even when tension is considerable, but in difficult tasks only a small amount of anxiety is needed to cripple performance.

Anxiety is thus to some degree useful and is occasionally experienced by everyone. It can be mild or severe depending on circumstances and personality characteristics, but all people, though varying in proneness to anxiety, can be incapacitated if a threatening environment is thrust upon them for a prolonged period. During intense combat, all soldiers will eventually show disabling anxiety if the situation is protracted[17].

Anxiety is distinguished from fear only by convention, with *fear* being the term for a transient, intense, and focused response to a particular and immediate threat and *anxiety* the term for a more sustained and variable emotion developed in the face of a more subtly threatening situation. Anxiety's earliest manifestations are a sense of vigilance and tension, features bringing with them alertness and a sense of stimulation that are not necessarily unpleasant. They are an aspect of excitement, can be sought out in a spirit of adventure, and their discharge and relief, for example, in a successful performance, can be a source of enjoyment[121].

With increasing anxiety, however, dysphoric qualities increase. All efforts become fatiguing and chronic tiredness is a regular complaint. Tension, vigilance, and arousal give way to worry, agitation, distractibility, jumpiness, depersonalization, and loss of efficiency; autonomic features of anxiety, such as tachycardia, stomach cramps, and dry mouth, add considerably to the dysphoria. There is also a sense of being unable to fill the lungs, with consequent overbreathing, which may increase the sense of depersonalization with feelings of light-headedness and floating and which occasionally even induces tetany. The final result is an incapacitated and demoralized person in severe distress.

Dysphoric anxiety demands resolution, but suitable resolutions vary with circumstances and individuals. Obviously the most immediate way of eliminating anxiety is to leave the situation and to avoid it in the future. This is only occasionally the most realistic solution. It is impossible, for example, to run from combat without risking new dangers or to leave a job without disrupting other commitments. Effective teaching diminishes the severity of occupational anxiety and should eventually replace it with the enjoyment of skill, a phenomenon recognized by teachers everywhere. Effective leadership in battle can modify the intensity of anxiety by similarly increasing skill, confidence, and *esprit de corps*. Here, mastery of the situation rather than its avoidance removes anxiety. This is a very successful way of managing anxiety, but it implies the reassessment of what is at first a threatening situation and the discovery of means to eliminate its threatening potential. This task is not easy, so it is scarcely surprising that most of us at various times require help from others to accomplish it.

Avoidance and mastery are ideal solutions to anxiety. When they are unavailable or must be deferred, any of several other modes of dealing with the emotion itself may appear. These modes are attempts to modify anxiety as an experience. Thus, some people discover that sedatives like alcohol reduce tension, a discovery that brings temporary relief but also carries with it the risk of sedative abuse if anxiety is chronic. People can also deal with anxiety (and particularly its unpleasant feelings of weakness) by replacing it with another, more active state, such as anger or aggression. These transformations often occur so unconsciously that the individual may be unaware that anxiety is involved at all. The experience and expression of anxiety can be altered in many other ways, but in each case there are contributions from the individual, the situation, past experience, and sociocultural expectations.

These various influences will determine not only whether anxiety is mastered but also whether the anxious person becomes a patient. The Dohrenwends and their colleagues have shown that many people in the general population have emotional distress indistinguishable in degree and kind from that reported by psychiatric patients[122]. Such people may not seek professional help, in part because they are not, in Frank's term, demoralized by their suffering[123], or because their social networks are such that the assistance of family and friends is sufficient aid, or perhaps because their cultural perspectives do not acknowledge the problem as one needing a physician's attention[124].

The mental state of anxiety is not difficult to recognize. Although it can also occur as part of a discrete disorder with a genetic basis (phobic anxiety

syndrome), an understandable linkage between the emotion and its provocation can usually be described by the patient and appreciated by the examiner.
The relationship of potential, provocation, and response in anxiety has been
studied empirically and is one of the classical examples of reasoning about
mental states as forms and functions [125].

This close look at anxiety can be repeated for a series of other states of
mind in which the paradigm of personality, provocation, and response can be
appreciated. In each of these states of mind, the links are those of meaning
between a subject/agent, a particular situation, and an emotional response
that is abnormal in degree but not in form. The application of these paradigms
to given individuals presents an understandable set of relationships on which
modes of intervention may be built. In the anxious personality faced with
circumstances he perceives as threatening, we can understand the appearance
of panic and even alcoholism. In the same way, for the self-dramatizing,
extraverted, and emotionally labile individual called histrionic, we understand
how an environment perceived as neglectful can provoke anger, depression,
and self-injurious behavior. The self-doubting, perfectionistic, and introverted
person, in a situation viewed as changing and unsettled, risks the development
of anxiety, frustration, and obsessions. The affectionless and adventure-seeking
personality in a poorly organized environment may manifest the behavior of
delinquency, whereas an unstable, aggressive individual in threatening circumstances may become violent. These are paradigms of regular occurrence,
and their treatment forms a large part of psychiatric practice.

If we apply this method of understanding to reactive emotional states we
can see that they have several characteristics. First, the central issue is an
exaggeration of a normal emotional response. Second, the patients are distinguished in a quantitative rather than a qualitative way from normal individuals. Thus, although we are all capable of emotional responses, we are not
all neurotic, because most of our responses are appropriate in degree and in
duration to the events that provoke them.

Third, causation for the difficulty is both meaningful and multiple; it rests
on linkages between such features as inherited characteristics, early life experiences, physical health, and situational stresses. The same symptoms may
appear in different situations for different individuals because it is the perceived
environment that provokes the response.

Fourth, diagnosis, too, is individual and depends on the appreciation of a
multiplicity of different features in a given patient, including an assessment of
his strengths as well as his vulnerabilities, the threats perceived, and the responses that result. This is a formulation rather than a label. Diseases are
categories that fit well into a labeling nosology; here, in neurotic reactions, a
paragraph is needed for each patient.

Fifth, in neurotic patients prognosis is uncertain for two reasons: personality traits tend to provide enduring vulnerabilities; and circumstances, important in provoking, maintaining, and relieving the emotional state, are often unpredictable.

Finally, therapy must be tailor-made for each patient despite symptomatic similarity. Although two people complain of depression, one may be a dependent and self-dramatizing elderly widow in poor health who must move from her daughter's house, while the other is a perfectionistic and self-doubting adolescent who has left home for difficult college work. Although they share certain emotional complaints, their personalities and situations are so dissimilar that the goals and methods of achieving insight, environmental change, and symptom relief may be quite different. Common to helping both, however, will be an appreciation of the meaningful nature of the links between emotion and its provocations, the contribution of personality, the need to develop a supportive relationship in treatment, and some decision about which goals are possible for this individual in these circumstances. Does she need and can she be prepared for radical insight, change, and new acceptance, or would she be better provided with simpler tactics to resolve the present situation and restore her equilibrium?

Whether one will attempt to modify the patient's vulnerability, ameliorate the distress provoked by his current situation, or teach him how to avoid psychologically damaging situations in the future depends on many aspects of an individual presentation. But it is clear that we are not speaking here about cure in the sense of a disease eradicated so much as guidance for people vulnerable to circumstances.

This is a context for the explanation of neurotic states. It rests on an appreciation of the connections linking potentials, provocations, and responses — connections that do not take the form of biological laws and do not act to compel an identical response in every instance. These connections lack such powerful predictive force and are in fact not intended for prediction. They are developed to provide a mode for understanding people in emotional difficulty.

The relationships between potentials, provocations, and responses are meaningful rather than determinative. We grasp their significance from our capacity to appreciate or empathize with them. They are individual in that, although plausible for all, they are actual only in particular instances. They are dynamic in that they represent an interactive group of processes which includes motives and opportunities, they are open to many influences, and they are capable of many alternative expressions. They find their persuasive power in their apparently comprehensive grasp of a multitude of issues arising from within and impinging from without upon a particular patient.

IV

THE CONCEPT
OF BEHAVIORS

13

The Concept of Motivation in Relation to Behaviors

There is a large and heterogeneous group of psychiatric conditions that are difficult to categorize even though they are commonly seen in psychiatric practice and share a number of characteristics. This group includes such problems as alcoholism, suicide, anorexia nervosa, delinquency, and drug abuse. Despite their obvious differences, these conditions are similar in that in each a decision is taken to engage in a particular activity. Further, each raises questions about the criteria for clinical abnormality and thus about the suitability of classifying it as a medical condition. Even the term *condition* can be seen as prejudging this issue, because attitudes about such activities derive almost as much from social expectations, institutions, and values as they do from the biological and psychological sciences and because treatment depends so much on persuasion that it may seem more like social control than medical therapy.

Although each of these conditions may be profitably viewed as a separate issue, the group they form has a fundamental unity, and the recognition of this commonality renders more comprehensible the whole group of conditions and the controversy that surrounds each of them. These activities, despite their differences, are all examples of behaviors—that is, of activities designated by their consequences.

Behavior, defined in this way, means more than activity, more than coordinated sensorimotor events; it implies the concept of a goal that gives the activity its meaning in the context of the behaving individual's circumstances. Sometimes the dominance of the activity by the purposive behavior will be obvious and clearly comprehended by the subject; at other times the subject will not be able to define his goal, though others may infer it from the consequences of the activity on that occasion and in that setting. Behavior is a construct that makes sense out of observations of activity and activity's regularities.

Perhaps the best way to make the conceptual and methodological issues in this perspective clear is to recount a regular occurrence in nature rather than in psychopathology. The California gray whale lives for most of the year in the region of the Bering Straits. Each winter, however, it begins a migration of thousands of miles along the North American coast to the Baja Peninsula. In the warm lagoons of that portion of California the animals breed and bear young and then, in early spring, travel again thousands of miles back to their northern habitat.

In the course of the migration the animals display many activities—swimming, spouting, chasing, sounding—and an observer who saw them for only a brief time would not be aware of the ultimate domination of their activities by goal-directed migratory behavior. That domination lies hidden unless the animals are observed over time and their eventual destination and the regular recurrence of the migratory behavior are seen.

The whales are not just swimming; they are migrating. Explanations are needed for this behavioral construct—migration—which directs and modifies the activity of the swimming animal so that it reaches its destination. Behavior, in this sense, is a construct that acknowledges a purpose behind certain of the regularities to be observed in activity. As a construct, the reliability of the observations can be challenged. So can the validity of the construct as an explanation of the regular features being observed. But, crucially, the construct gives a focus for descriptive and explanatory efforts that would not be undertaken if only the motor-sensory activity of the animal was considered.

Human beings employ many coordinations of hand, eye, and mouth, but we recognize and distinguish among them the behavior of eating, in which the activity leads to the consequence of food consumption. Eating is a clear and specific behavior, even though its particular appearance on any occasion may vary depending on the state of the organism, the availability of nutrients, personal attitudes toward food, and social custom. Yet even though the behavior can be performed under differing circumstances and can be disturbed in certain ways (for example, overeating, undereating, pica), it is clear that we are always considering manifestations of the same phenomenon—the behavior of eating—and that an understanding of the behavior, whether normal or abnormal, must consider issues ranging from the biological to the cultural.

We believe that the other conditions mentioned above represent behaviors in much the same sense, that they are activities defined by their consequences and appearing in various guises. The concept of behavior as a category (albeit a large and heterogeneous one) provides answers to a number of questions commonly asked of psychiatrists: What is hysteria? (It is a behavior in which the symptoms and signs of disease are imitated); Is homosexuality a disease? (No, it is not; it is a behavior); What is the treatment for a person with suicidal tendencies? (Because suicidal behavior can arise in several circumstances, its treatment depends on those circumstances and thus ranges from psychotherapy for demoralization to electroconvulsive therapy for manic-depressive illness).

The recognition of the category of behaviors brings with it an advantage of all categorical designations: identification. Each member of the category is thus seen to share certain common issues, chief among which is the relationship of behaviors to body, mind, and custom.

With identification comes the need for explanation. How is it that people behave in this way? The *what* question answered by identification is followed by the *how* question of the mechanisms that produce the behavior and the *why* question of the intentions of the individual who manifests it. We have problems with both aspects of explanation, and our analysis includes issues of both form and function.

To begin, there is little information about the fundamental mechanisms producing any behavior in any organism, let alone in human beings. Although our knowledge of the nervous system is quite advanced in its comprehension of the integrative functioning of the motor-sensory apparatus that makes it possible for the organism to produce coordinated movements, our knowledge of the mechanisms that direct this apparatus and enable the organism to select goals and to adapt to changing circumstances—the very features that differentiate the construct *behavior* from mere activity and may be the most essential characteristic of animal life—is sparse, though these mechanisms are the focus of much neuroscience research today.

In many ways, that research has important roots in the work of Freud, whose most lasting contribution to the field of psychology may be his having pointed out that human beings are driven by motivations that often dominate their activity and appear in various forms. In *Project for a Scientific Psychology,* Freud noted:

> With an (increasing) complexity of the interior (of the organism), the nervous system receives stimuli from the somatic element itself—endogenous stimuli—which have equally to be discharged. These have their origin in the cells of the body and give rise to the major needs: hunger, respiration, sexuality. From these the organism cannot withdraw as it does from external stimuli. . . . They only cease subject to particular conditions, which must be realized in the external world. (Cf., for instance, the need for nourishment.) In order to accomplish such an action . . . an effort is required . . . since the individual is being subjected to conditions which may be described as *the exigencies of life* [126].

These "endogenous stimuli" are the precursors of Freud's *Trieb,* often translated as *instinct* but perhaps better read as *drive.* Thus, in *Instincts and Their Vicissitudes,* Freud defined instincts in the following ways:

> a concept on the frontier between the mental and the somatic, as the psychical representative of the stimuli originating from within the organism and reaching

the mind, as a measure of the demand made upon the mind for work in consequence of its connection with the body.

We are now in a position to discuss certain terms which are used in reference
to the concept of an instinct—for example, its "pressure", its "aim", its "object"
and its "source".

By the pressure (*Drang*) of an instinct we understand its motor factor, the
amount of force or the measure of the demand for work which it represents.
The characteristic of exercising pressure is common to all instincts; it is in fact
their very essence. . . .

The aim (*Ziel*) of an instinct is in every instance satisfaction, which can only be
obtained by removing the state of stimulation at the source of the instinct. But although the ultimate aim of each instinct remains unchangeable, there may yet
be different paths leading to the same ultimate aim; so that an instinct may be
found to have various nearer or intermediate aims, which are combined or inter-
changed with one another. . . .

The object (*Objekt*) of an instinct is the thing in regard to which or through
which the instinct is able to achieve its aim. It is what is most variable about an
instinct and is not originally connected with it, but becomes assigned to it only in
consequence of being peculiarly fitted to make satisfaction possible. The object
is not necessarily something extraneous: it may equally well be a part of the subject's own body. It may be changed any number of times in the course of the vicissitudes which the instinct undergoes during its existence. . . .

By the source (*Quelle*) of an instinct is meant the somatic process which occurs
in an organ or part of the body and whose stimulus is represented in mental life
by an instinct. We do not know whether this process is invariably of a chemical
nature or whether it may also correspond to the release of other, e.g. mechanical,
forces. . . . Although instincts are wholly determined by their origin in a somatic
source, in mental life we know them only by their aims. An exact knowledge of
the sources of an instinct is not invariably necessary for purposes of psychological
investigation; sometimes its source may be inferred from its aim [127].

It is the beauty and thoroughness of this description that identified the
concepts of behavior and motivation in clinical science. The construct behavior proposes that behind the activities of the organism are goals toward
which those activities are moving, directly or indirectly, consciously or unconsciously. From observations of the activities and the regular achievement
of the goals the hidden dominance of behavior is construed. The goals vary;
hence, behaviors differ in character. As constructs, however, behaviors are
discriminated from simple activity by being goal-directed and from each other
by their differing goals.

Freud adduced a motivated quality for all behaviors and believed that
motivations are hidden in much psychopathology. To examine this position it
is necessary to consider the characteristics of the basic motivated behaviors.

14

Characteristics of
Motivated Behaviors

$\mathbf{M}$otivated behaviors may be characterized in several ways. They can be designated according to their specificity, from behaviors with quite general features (such as the activity rhythm, waxing and waning in relation to time of day and novelty of the environment) to those having more specific characteristics (such as defense, manifested as either fight or flight in response to threat) to very stereotyped behaviors (such as feeding, drinking, and sexual behaviors, in which consummatory consequences are evident).

These behaviors have an adaptive function. They relate in a hierarchy, one superseding the other in a variety of situations so that the organism is seldom locked into a dangerous activity by the domination of an inappropriate motivation. Inhibition is as critical as excitation, and it is the combination of the two that renders the motivated state a variable and intermittent manifestation.

Although motivated behaviors are often elicited by external stimuli, these stimuli vary in power from occasion to occasion. The same visual and olfactory stimuli that prompt feeding after a period of fasting are devoid of interest following a meal. Sexually provocative signals arouse adults, but are less intriguing to children. There are thus both temporary and long-standing changes in responsiveness to behavior-provoking stimuli, and it is this changing responsiveness that is at the heart of the phenomenon of motivation.

Motivated behaviors are also provoked by internal changes, and they are therefore tied to visceral and endocrine phenomena, with the limbic-hypothalamic system as an important neural site of organization and integration.

In humans, some aspects of the motivated behaviors can be appreciated through the self-reports of individuals behaving in particular ways. The domination of activity by motivational states, which in animals is provoked by means such as deprivation and hormone injections, is reported by people as sensitivity to stimuli, craving for experience, or distraction from other activity. The best example of this phenomenon may be the emergence of sexual interests and activities during puberty, so that stimuli previously only mildly interesting become arousing and preoccupying.

The goal of sexual expression must find a balance between personal needs and social customs. The ability to find this balance usually improves with experience, making the behavior both efficient and acceptable. Under certain conditions the expression can only be partial, a compromise that yields some satisfaction and the temporary inhibition of the sense of drive, domination, and interest.

Sexually motivated behavior can, therefore, be described as both a search for pleasure and a demand for release from tension. Both aspects appear to occur simultaneously and both have been built into theories (for example, pleasure principle; drive reduction) as postulates for the ultimate goal of all behaviors. From a phenomenological point of view, however, the main elements are the sense of interest and responsiveness, which can become dominant if deprivation is prolonged, and the temporary reduction of interest and activity that follows a consummatory expression.

Much the same kind of phenomenological description can be given for motivated behaviors other than sexual ones — eating, drinking, sleeping — with the added point that any one behavior with prolonged deprivation of its aim can replace all the others and that much of a person's energy can become committed to this single aim until it has been accomplished. With behaviors such as eating and drinking, which are essential to life, prolonged deprivation can lead to the abandonment of other interests and to the neglect of efforts to accommodate the behavior to socially learned principles.

The expression of all of these behaviors is accompanied by a subjectively appreciated state of interest. The behavior can be modified by circumstance, by experience, by reflection on the subtleties of its arousal, by the manner in which it is pursued, and by the particulars of its expression. Both the state of mind and the behavior expressed can be felt by the individual as related to his interests and activities, emerging as an aspect of his will and pointing to a course of action.

Thus, the variety in the particular manifestations of motivated behaviors can derive from many sources in any given individual. These sources of variation merely shape the expression of the behavior, however, reconciling it to the capacities of the individual and to the demands of circumstances. The variety is in the approach; the consummatory act is ultimately stereotyped. In the end, the pig and the parson both eat.

Not all motivated behaviors as we have defined them appear in human beings with the simple appetitive approach and consummatory termination that characterize the basic drives. Interests, activities, and satisfactions of a subtler kind, which are developed cognitively and socially and which rest on man's capacity for symbolic elaboration and his social nature, can also be seen. These include the behaviors of the scholar, artist, collector, leader, explorer, and creator. Although components of such activities may be derived from basic drives, they can be appreciated as phenomena in themselves; as meaningful examples of human aspirations rather than only as the vestigial manifestations of evolutionary mechanisms; as disguised expressions of repressed desires; or merely as the result of a chain of stimulus and response. Though a reductionistic approach to these behaviors has lost favor in psychiatric practice, it still informs the application (and misapplication) of psychiatric theory to biography, history, and critical interpretation.

Behaviors must be distinguished from simple reflexes that occur automatically as responses to stimuli, but it is equally important that they be seen as more pressing and determinative than casual choices from among attractive alternatives. A motivated behavior is not like a reflex action because its provocative stimuli are very far from stereotyped and can vary in power from occasion to occasion. In fact, this variation in the power of an identical stimulus from occasion to occasion is a hallmark of motivated states. The same plate of food that appeared so attractive prior to a meal is devoid of such qualities immediately afterward. The behavioral expression can be suppressed, either by its replacement with activities that are incompatible with it or through the conscious refusal to engage in the behavior despite its insistence. Such a refusal may derive from any of a number of other motives tied to human values, culture, and meaning; examples include celibacy among the clergy, the ascetic denials of religious ceremony (for example, those associated with Yom Kippur, Lent, Ramadan), and even the self-starvation of political prisoners. It is clear from the study of man that these motivated behaviors are not simple actions that will always be expressed as direct elements of the "wiring" of the nervous system; they also respond to psychological and social forces.

The drive behind motivated behaviors is far from trivial, unlike that behind the choice between pleasant alternatives. A person's interests become progressively more dominated by aspects of a motivation, a domination reflected in his preoccupations, his dreaming, and eventually in some aspects of his activity. The sense of choice may remain, but it is progressively narrowed as the drive increases. There may be no actual irresistible impulse in the sense that a tendon jerk is irresistible, but there can certainly be a growing urge to act that can become so intense that its expression has almost a forced quality.

Motivated behaviors are a vital aspect of human life. They can form the source of psychopathology both in the aberration of their goals and in the distress they bring to individuals driven by them.

15

Characteristics of Abnormal Behaviors

In clinical settings, disturbed behaviors can usually be accounted for by abnormalities in the strength of the urge, the mode of its expression, or the nature of its object. In some patients, however, the problem lies not so much with the characteristics of the motivation itself as with other aspects of the individual and his circumstances. Included here could be the distress provoked in a mentally subnormal person by the appearance of sexuality with puberty, especially if the customary paths to sexual expression are thought inappropriate for that person or if he is lacking in social skills. Similarly, the homosexual behavior of certain prisoners can often be appreciated as arising from an obstruction to heterosexual expression in the prison environment. It is likely, however, that examples such as these constitute the minority of behavioral problems needing explanation and treatment. More common are those behaviors that emerge in individuals who have no obvious deficits or special constraints, behaviors that raise the issues of what should be called abnormal and what should therefore be a legitimate topic for psychiatric practice.

Occasionally the answer seems obvious. Self-injury and suicide may be considered disturbed behaviors by the identification of the goal itself, as might alcohol consumption when it is carried to the point of physical dependence, bodily illness, and personal dilapidation. Yet even this opinion must occasionally be defended in a society that asks such questions as, Whose life is it, anyway?

The major source of explanatory difficulty here rests with the nature of the behaviors themselves. They are generally graded phenomena—not so much either present or absent as they are manifest in varying degrees. Individuals who display a particular problematic behavior show it to a greater or lesser extent and merge imperceptibly into the population that shows little or none of it. There are many illustrations of this phenomenon. Alcohol consumption, for example, is very common in the adult population of the United States, yet the abuse of alcohol varies from the rare intoxication of the many to the continuous drunkenness, ill health, and progressive addiction of the few. What is to be called alcoholism and who an alcoholic is therefore problematic.

Similar gradations in the population are obvious for other behaviors, such as gambling, drug abuse, and delinquency. In the case of sexual behavior, Kinsey and his associates proposed a formal dimension ranging from exclusive heterosexuality at one end to exclusive homosexuality at the other[128]. Behaviors are thus dimensional phenomena in the population, but because clinical diagnoses are couched in categorical terms (for example, alcoholism, hysteria), the point at which abnormality is identified—where the dimensional becomes the categorical—may seem here, as in the study of personality, a difficult and arbitrary judgment.

One unsatisfactory but at least logically consistent way of defining abnormality for some of these behaviors rests on their social nature. Because they involve actions in society, they can be the subjects of laws. The inability of a person to conform his behavior to the constraints of law identifies him as needing society's assistance, perhaps from its physicians. Yet the difficulties with such a view are many. This approach can leave the decision of whether or not a particular behavior is abnormal in a medical sense to the vagaries of the political process. The abuse of legal definitions of abnormality in behavior can lead to a situation similar to that in some totalitarian states, in which laws have been used to stigmatize as mentally ill persons engaging in political activities that challenge the state.

A second and somewhat better criterion for regarding a behavior as a matter for clinical concern is the judgment as to whether the individual in question or others suffer from its expression. This is a handy standard and is exemplified by the issue of alcohol consumption. Such an approach rests on objectively observable disruptions in the health, work, and relationships of individuals, disruptions that identify persons as being in trouble because of the behavior. Yet even the judgment that an injury is present can be value laden, at least in borderline conditions.

A final and usually persuasive criterion of abnormality is a distortion of the behavior itself, such as when it takes the form of a stereotyped "craving" for a particular experience. Under these circumstances it can often be appreciated that the behavior is now divorced from the coordinated biological, psychological, and social elements that customarily lead to its satisfying and acceptable expression. The craving focuses on some portion of the activity and provokes an intensely developed interest in that alone.

Such cravings can be relatively benign—for example, the desires of a pregnant woman for an unusual food, desired not for its nutrient value but for some other and seemingly irresistible quality. More distressing and potentially difficult are sexual cravings, in which particular sexual activities become the sole focus of interest, dominating all other considerations of sexual expression, including a sense of affection for and bonding to the partner. The actions become ritualized, stereotyped, and demanding and are often expressed despite considerable danger to the individual experiencing the craving. Still more obvious in its sense of domination of the life of the person is the craving found in addiction to drugs or alcohol. Here the justification for medical intervention is the attempt to free someone from the enslavement of the craving. A craving is not only stronger and more difficult to control than other motivated states, but, as Jaspers points out, it is often experienced as something alien and compelling whose expression produces only temporary relief and few of the natural accompaniments of the behavior as normally seen[129].

This quality—craving—may confidently be regarded as a criterion of abnormality and is exemplified in some of the sexual perversions; in the morbid fear of obesity in anorexia nervosa; in the bulimic episodes of some individuals with eating disorders; in the alcohol and drug dependency syndromes; and even in a craving for symbolic experience, as in the behavior of patients with factitious disorders (Munchausen syndrome) who injure themselves to gain admission to hospitals. The power of the craving is evident in its domination of both the patient's behavior and his mental experiences, and many individuals with cravings can contrast them in quality and quantity to their normal motivations. In fact, the patient often defines himself as abnormal because he is distressed and overmastered. Cravings constitute the best evidence for behavioral abnormality in the categorical sense.

It is now perhaps evident why the issues of mechanism and etiology in the area of behavior are so problematic. The questions of explanation, the *how* questions (How was that behavior provoked?) intermingle with *why* questions (Why did he want to behave in that way?), an intermingling that often leads to confused reasoning. For example, the cause of a sexual act can be addressed in terms of hormonal activation, sensory stimuli, previous reinforcements, and present circumstances and can lead to a *how* explanation couched in terms of probability and of necessary and sufficient causes. An equally satisfying answer might explain the behavior in question as the desire of the actor, for whom the act has a meaning comprehensible in terms of his personality, relationships, fantasy life, environment, mood, and intentions. This *why* answer would take its sense of confidence from the empathic appeal of a plausible, meaningful understanding of a particular individual at a certain moment in his life.

There is great value in both approaches to explanation, and in any given patient the most adequate explanation must take from both of them for completeness. In one approach behavior is viewed as a form of human activity, to be correlated with biological, psychological, and sociological variables; in the other, behavior is understood in a meaningful way, as serving a comprehensible function for the individual observed. It is useful to consider first the question of how behaviors are produced in the population in general and then the question of why an individual behaves in a particular way.

16

Behaviors as Forms

Perhaps more than many other issues in psychiatry, behaviors may legitimately be thought of in terms of forms. Most behaviors are publicly ascertainable and depend less on communication than on observation. It is thus possible to begin with an approach to behavior that might clarify the legitimate questions of confidence about just how much of the population variation for a behavior may be accounted for by certain causes and mechanisms.

A fundamental cause of behavior for all organisms is the gene. It is at the genetic level, for instance, that the programming of normal development begins, and with it the formation of neural structures that serve functions like eating and sleeping as well as the timing of stages, such as puberty, that are important in sexual behavior. The interplay of natural selection and genetics can be appreciated in the homeostatic features of basic motivated behaviors like feeding, in which caloric intake tends to be sustained at a set level, though modified appropriately for activity, ambient temperature, and other factors.

Disruption of the brain itself can disturb the natural expression of genetically derived mechanisms, but they normally function smoothly for the benefit of the organism. It is only in rare conditions like the Prader-Willi syndrome, with its chromosomal abnormality, overeating, and obesity, or the Lesch-Nyhan syndrome, with its recessive inheritance and self-injury, that we can see particular disturbances in basic behaviors which rest on genetic defects. Though in these disorders the correlation of phenotype to genome is clear, the relationship of genetic mechanisms to specific behaviors is usually less evident.

When we consider the genetic contribution to various behaviors we usually have in mind issues such as alcoholism, delinquency, and homosexuality, behaviors in which not only is the phenotypic expression so graded in the population that its confident identification in all examples is both difficult and

111

disputed, but it is also so dependent on a variety of environmental influences that any genetic contribution might be difficult to discern and would be questioned if proposed.

Certainly it has not so far been possible to find Mendelian heredity patterns in these behaviors. Behavioral categories are usually so heterogeneous and disjunctive that such patterns might be obscured by a mixture of causes among their members, but twin, family, population, and adoption studies have all been employed to reveal by indirect inference some genetic role in each of the behavioral categories studied. Kallmann, for example, found a concordance rate of 100 percent in male monozygotic twins, one of whom was identified as homosexual, while the rate for male dizygotic twins was much less[130]. In a later systematic survey of the literature, Heston and Shields concluded that the concordance rate was closer to 50 percent for monozygotic twins[131]; still an impressive figure if homosexual behavior were regarded as determined purely by environment and choice. Slater and Cowie proposed that in the Europeo-American culture of the present era genetic factors play some role in the production of homosexual behavior, but they also point out that sexual behavior is molded by many influences, including "acquired tastes" closely related to the culture in which the individual develops[132]. Thus, in ancient Greece, where homosexuality was not considered a deviation, the genetic contribution to the behavior was submerged within cultural mores. It is possible, Slater and Cowie point out, to picture a future in which homosexual behavior will be so much in the cultural experience of every individual that the genetic contribution will become undetectable.

Very similar methods, results, and reasoning apply to the contribution of genetics to the elucidation of criminal behavior and delinquency. That there is a genetic contribution was powerfully evidenced by Johannes Lange in his study of twins, published with the fearsome title *Crime as Destiny*. In this study, only three of thirteen monozygotic pairs were discordant for criminal records, whereas only two of seventeen dizygotic same-sex pairs were concordant[133]. A more recent, population-based study by Christiansen of nearly 6,000 twin pairs yielded lower concordance rates for monozygotic twins (35.8 percent for monozygotic pairs versus 12.3 percent for dizygotic twinships) than had been observed by Lange and other early workers using selected samples, but an important hereditary contribution is still suggested[134].

Studies demonstrating a genetic factor in criminality have also acknowledged environmental influences. For example, in the twin study of Rosanoff, Handy, and Plesset, though a higher concordance rate for adult criminality was again found in male monozygotic twin pairs when compared to male dizygotic pairs, the rate for juvenile delinquency was quite similar for monozygotic and dizygotic groups[135]. These results suggest that influences such as the home, school, or neighborhood play the major role in provoking juvenile delinquency, whereas hereditary factors may be more crucial in the development of later, adult crime.

A similar interaction of genetic and environmental effects has also been observed using the adoption-study technique. Hutchings and Mednick, for example, found that although hereditary factors seemed to be more influential in promoting criminal behavior in male adoptees, both nature and nurture play a role[136]:

	Number of Adoptees	Percentage Criminal
Neither biological nor *adoptive father criminal*	333	10.4
Adoptive father criminal	52	11.2
Biological father criminal	219	21.0
Both fathers criminal	58	36.2

A genetic contribution to alcoholism was discerned in the family studies of Manfred Bleuler[137]. The objection that alcoholism might be simply the result of shared family life rather than of shared genes has been answered at least in part by the systematic adoption studies of Goodwin and his colleagues, which demonstrated that the sons of alcoholics raised by unrelated, non-alcoholic adoptive parents were four times likelier to become alcoholic than were adopted-out sons of nonalcoholics[138]. This work, confirmed in other studies[139], indicates that a specific susceptibility to alcoholism rather than to other psychiatric disorders, including antisocial behavior, is transmitted from parent to child, even if the child is not exposed to the alcoholic parent.

Such studies are indicators of a role for genetics in these and presumably other behavioral disorders. What is also clear is that the mechanisms for such genetic actions have yet to be explained. Even when a specific, genetically determined enzyme defect is known, as in the Lesch-Nyhan syndrome, how that defect is related to a particular behavior is not understood. In other instances, what is inherited may not be a mechanism specific to a behavior but rather something related to qualities of that person which render him more vulnerable to social influences. Thus, in certain environments, one's bodily habitus may make one more attractive to homosexual encouragement or more likely to be sought out for the strength and agility required for certain active criminal pursuits.

Without the clear indications offered by Mendelian characteristics, the genetic contribution to behavioral disorders as presently defined is most likely polygenic. In such a case the additive effects of a large number of genes modify the impact on the individual of family and cultural forces, which shape his development, reinforce his inclinations, and provide his milieu. That genes have a role in behavior can be demonstrated; that behaviors are influenced by other forces, particularly those of the social world, can also be demonstrated.

There is a great deal of evidence that cultural forces play important roles in many behaviors and that they do so by several different modes of action. The most obvious way that such forces act is by providing opportunities for the expression of behaviors. For instance, the eighteenth-century British political decisions to encourage local distillers of gin and to raise taxes on the imported product made highly concentrated grain alcohol available to large numbers of people at low cost, an availability that was a major contribution to an increase in the prevalence of alcohol abuse[140]. With a rise in alcohol-related problems came the temperance movement (vigorously supported by psychiatrists such as Kraepelin, Eugen Bleuler, and Adolf Meyer), a social force that was effective in leading several countries to restrict the distribution of alcohol. This resulted in a sharp, though temporary, decrease in the consequences of alcohol abuse during Prohibition in the United States and after the introduction of licensing laws in Great Britain during World War I.

But society, besides providing an opportunity for the expression of behavior, can actually incite it. Thus, alcohol consumption, smoking, and early sexual behavior can be encouraged by such socially important phenomena as peer pressure, advertising, and the provision of role models. Is there any parent who does not sometimes despair of his or her ability to influence a child's behavior in the face of these forces?

Finally, more general social conditions can affect the expression of several behaviors at once. Emil Durkheim, the first major student of sociology to examine the factors provoking suicide, found that this behavior was more common among people who were poorly integrated into their cultures, and that such distressing social forces as poverty and isolation seemed to encourage both suicide and delinquency[141].

The problem with resting the etiology of behavioral disorders on cultural and social forces alone is that these forces act on many members of the community, only a few of whom demonstrate the behavior in question. Unless some appreciation of personal vulnerability is also provided, the development of a behavioral disorder in any given individual cannot be understood.

The Gluecks demonstrated that in the delinquent population there are clear personality characteristics that can be used to predict to some extent which individuals in particular social environments will become delinquent[142]. From early childhood, delinquent individuals can be seen to be assertive, self-centered, adventure-seeking, easily bored, and explosive individuals who tend to be limit-testing and suspicious of authority. These characteristics make them more prone to take up activities that challenge society's rules and standards. The Gluecks point out a sharp distinction between those individuals and others in the very same family and culture who do not become delinquent despite experiencing the same social disruptions. The outstanding characteristics of nondelinquent individuals are a sense of concern about others' appraisal of their conduct, a capacity for guilt, and an ability to worry over consequences that is exhibited in all aspects of their lives, not just in relation to law. It is therefore impossible to consider social and cultural forces as sufficient causes for a particular behavior in a given individual. It is likely, however, that they are among the more important determinants of the number of people expressing and troubled by a particular behavior, because with increasing social pressure less and less vulnerability is required to provoke that behavior.

If genetic and social elements combine to provoke behaviors, they do so in a developing and experiencing person. The concept of development gives a perspective relating genetic to psychological and social causes and a means of partitioning these causes over a lifetime. It is important to appreciate not only that development influences behavior but that it does so sequentially, so that a given event at one stage shapes the expression of later development, behavior, and experience.

Organisms other than *Homo sapiens* have quite strict periods in which behaviorally important events must occur for later species-specific behaviors to appear normally. The critical period and imprinting displayed in such animals as dogs and birds are examples of these phenomena.

In human beings, the evidence is less compelling that such critical or sensitive periods exist. Money and his associates note that gender identity is established in early infancy and affects later sexual behavior in a crucial fashion[143]. Bowlby employs an ethological concept of attachment to explain the natural development of parental bonds, which, if disrupted early in life, can be hard to replace later [144]. Yet none of these concepts has the determinism of critical periods in animals, and all have been challenged by other observations.

It is well established that biological events have an important influence on human behavior when they occur at particular stages in development. For example, though the formation of male gender identity and behavior is influenced by sociocultural factors, prenatal exposure of the brain to androgens seems crucial in the process.

In normal males the Y chromosome initiates the production of androgens, imposing on the organism the program for male pituitary secretions and eventually for masculine sexual activity. Females, lacking the Y chromosome, follow a different course of development, but that course can be changed if females are exposed prenatally to androgens. Sometimes this occurs when their mothers are given progestin during pregnancy, but it can also happen in the adrenogenital syndrome, when the fetal adrenal gland produces an androgenic steriod rather than cortisol.

Money and Ehrhardt studied patients whose adrenogenital syndrome was diagnosed and treated early, so they looked like and were appropriately raised as girls[145]. In spite of the early treatment, however, many of them later chose play objects more traditionally associated with boys (guns, automobiles) than with girls (dolls), and preferred in their play to join boys in vigorous sports rather than to play with female friends, as control girls did.

Money and Ehrhardt have also studied males whose cells are insensitive to the androgens secreted by their testes [146]. These genetic males with the androgen-insensitivity syndrome respond to the relatively small amounts of circulating estrogen normally produced in males, and therefore they develop and seem to be, behaviorally as well as in their outward appearance, women.

The effects of hormonal changes on behavior are not limited to the fetal period. In normal puberty, behavior is altered, though in the direction prepared by previous development. In the patients studied by Imperato-McGinley and her associates, puberty produced or permitted a more fundamental change[147]. These patients were genetic males with a fetal deficiency of dihydrotestosterone, so they had ambiguous external genitalia and were brought up as girls. With the appearance of more obvious male features at puberty, however, they were able to shift to a masculine role, a behavioral change that prevailed over their gender of rearing. Thus, sexual identity and behavior do not rest simply on the individual's chromosomal constitution but also upon his particular developmental passage through a sequence that includes intrauterine hormonal exposure, gender attribution in early childhood, learning, and pubertal hormonal surges.

Although biological factors in development are of great interest, they seem to account for only a small number of patients seen with problematic behaviors. Patients who have not met developmental timetables that are based on sociocultural expectations can also have difficulties.

An interaction between genetic, developmental, and sociocultural factors is often required to explain and distinguish among behaviors that have superficial resemblances. School refusal is an example. Children can be brought to psychiatric attention because they do not willingly attend school, and though their behavior is the same, the underlying reasons are different. Some of these children are truants: they do not attend school, but neither do they stay home. They seek others of like mind and spend their time in play or sometimes in crime. Other children refuse school by staying home. These can be further differentiated into children who do so because they fear some aspect of the school situation (school phobia) and those who stay home because they fear leaving their mothers (separation anxiety). It is in this last group that we can find an immature child, whose dependent and often conflicted relationship with his mother is threatened by the necessity to meet a developmental schedule imposed by society. Though members of all these groups refuse to attend school, the underlying causes of and treatments for their behaviors are different, distinctions best reflected in the differing designations of each of the behaviors in the category.

Even if genetic mechanisms, developmental processes, and social influences have combined to produce the normal expression of a behavior, that expression may nonetheless be altered by the intervention of a disease process. In such cases the resulting behavioral abnormality is regarded as symptomatic of the disease state, because it appears and disappears with other manifestations of the illness. Thus, for example, homosexual behavior is occasionally seen in people only when they are suffering from mania. Their behavior under these circumstances is but one expression of the heightened sexual drive that sometimes accompanies the disorder and that may take other forms as well. Likewise, excessive consumption of alcohol, with all its physiological consequences, can occur in a manic patient experiencing an increase in all his appetites, although it never occurs when he is well.

It is crucial to recognize those examples of a behavior which are symptomatic of particular diseases, because the treatment of the behavior and its prognosis depend on the underlying cause. To mistake the suicidal behavior of a depressive individual who requires pharmacological treatment or electroconvulsive therapy for the self-injury provoked by romantic disappointment in a dependent and dramatic person who needs psychotherapeutic assistance is to overlook a fundamental distinction. Symptomatic behaviors are recognized by the company they keep with other symptoms, and the possibility of a relationship between disease and behavior should be considered in all cases.

That behaviors and diseases sometimes occur together raises the issue of whether certain behaviors should themselves be regarded as diseases. This position has been affirmed by several advocacy groups, especially those concerned with alcohol abuse.

The use of the term *disease* for alcohol abuse seems to us to be metaphorical: it signifies and dramatizes the craving over which some alcoholics apparently have no control. Though calling alcoholism a disease has had beneficial effects, including the improvement of society's attitudes about and services for alcoholics, to restrict our thinking about alcohol addiction to the disease concept may, in the long run, reduce our understanding of the behavior.

The disease concept progresses in a logical way from clinical syndrome to pathological disease state to etiological agency. It describes a process of reasoning as well as a set of facts. Though it might be applied to a syndrome like mania, in which alcohol abuse occurs, or to a subset of alcoholics who will someday be demonstrated to have a genetic defect that renders them vulnerable to addiction, the category of disease does not do justice to all of the varied manifestations and causes of excessive alcohol consumption.

It is the consumption of alcohol that is, after all, the *sine qua non* of alcoholism. Though that consumption can be an etiological factor leading to pathological disease states and clinical syndromes such as cirrhosis and delirium tremens, the drinking of alcohol, like the smoking of cigarettes, the avoidance of food, and the taking of poison, is itself a behavior. The addicted individual who is entrapped in a behavior prompted by a multiplicity of biological, physiological, and social forces is no less a victim than is a person with a disease that is provoked by some one necessary etiological agent; the disease concept, however, seeks only that single biological agent.

The perspective of behavior rather than of disease leads to an appreciation of the phenomena in question as the result of a dynamic interaction of many forces, including not only biological and sociological ones but also the attitudes and intentions of the behaving subjects themselves. To confine our reasoning about behaviors to the relatively narrow focus of the disease concept imposes conceptual restrictions that may interfere with our ability to understand and treat problematic behaviors. Behaviors can cause diseases and diseases can cause behaviors, but the terms are not interchangeable.

17

Behaviors as Functions

We have reviewed the ways in which a behavior depends on a neural apparatus built from the genetic constitution, how that behavior is responsive to hormonal and other biological influences, how it is modified by circumstances and sociocultural forces, and how it can be altered or provoked by disease. In these *how* explanations, though, the sense of meaning and purpose that is behavior's most obvious characteristic—the *why* explanation—has so far been ignored.

The sense of an agent intending to reach some desired goal remains a vital part of the phenomena of behavior. It is at least a challenge and often a rebuke to the adequacy of any explanation based on mechanisms and etiologies. How can we incorporate the experience of subjective insistence into our understanding of patients and their behavioral problems?

For the Freudians and all derivative psychodynamic theorists, drives *are* the explanation. Freud described and then incorporated drives into his theories of human behavior. The insistent quality of drive explained the resistance of mental disorders to change despite admonitions, advice, and experience. The pathological rigidity, implacability, and repetitiveness of the life stories of his patients could not come from choice, reason, or will, Freud argued, but are just what could arise from motivated drives, drives that are unacknowledged and disguised but nonetheless relentless and recurrent.

Sandor Lorand, in his explanation of the functions served and meanings revealed in the food refusal found in anorexia nervosa, presents a typical drive formulation:

The symptoms express the following meanings:

1) Loss of appetite: Food implies oral and sexual gratification identified with early phantasies of impregnation. Thus are revived strong feelings of guilt necessitating denial by rejection of food. Food usually is excessively charged with

119

importance in an environment where a patient develops anorexia nervosa. It is the vehicle of love and also of punishment. . . .

2) The denial of adulthood, in general and especially in sexuality: Adult problems cannot be handled because of constant preoccupation with the problems of food around which the earliest difficulties of the child centered. This preoccupation also excludes adult adjustment to sexual needs. Then too, genitality has to be denied because of desires and guilt centering around the early Oedipus relationship.

3) Wasting away: It expresses strong suicidal desires. . . .

4) Menstrual disturbances: Cessation of menstruation is an attempt to eliminate the problem of being preoccupied with genital function which in adulthood implies thoughts of sexual relationship and pregnancy. At times amenorrhea means permanent impregnation, and then again complete rejection of femininity. These are defenses against Oedipal guilt.

5) Guilt and atonement: Since the symptoms are used to obtain revenge and attention, they become charged with guilt, at the same time the suffering acts as expiatory self-punishment [148].

This is a remarkable stance. The conception of a hidden motivation behind the multiplicity of conscious acts is armed against objections because it undercuts reasoning itself. It gives a comprehensive functional meaning both to the sense of purpose experienced by the patient and to the pathological rigidity of his symptoms. It sustains the confidence of the therapist in his practice, whether he relieves the symptoms or not. Jung, Adler, and all the other schismatics break away from Freud over what constitutes the underlying, unconscious motivations, but the centrality of motivation itself remains in their reasoning. Methodologically they are the same; only the emphasis changes.

Clinical success may come from the encouragement these views give to sustaining and informing the psychotherapeutic relationship. When applied to individuals they cultivate an attitude that can be helpful and insightful. But the theorists overplay their hands when they generalize from particular patients to mankind. Then they make every action and capacity of human beings an expression of the identical motivation, a flowering of guises which attracts some by its explanatory display but which strains the credulity of others who see more choice and complexity in human affairs.

Behaviorists approach the function of behavior differently. Though they also acknowledge the phenomena of the motivated drives and may even credit Freud with discerning them, they propose that the subjective feature as well as the observable behavior must be explained. They reject as the answer to the question Why does he drink? the response Because he is thirsty, because it seems to make the explanation rest on an element that they consider part of the behavior itself.

Thus, B. F. Skinner, like other behaviorists, believes that all behaviors are ultimately the lawful and direct outcome of past experiences, but he sees this past experience in a more dynamic way than his predecessors [149]. Experience is not simply the regular occurrence of stimuli in temporal proximity to a re-sponse that is eventually conditioned to the stimuli—the original Pavlovian or classical conditioning paradigm. Rather, there is interaction between the organism and the environment such that actions (operants) of the organism that are at first no more than random, spontaneous elements from the or-ganism's behavioral repertoire (for example, pecking, pushing, scratching, biting) act upon the environment to provoke a change in it. This change can in turn affect the organism: it may provide food, make sound, cause pain. The environmental event thus acts as a reinforcement, increasing or decreasing the frequency of the initial behavioral operants; the environmental conse-quences "shape" the originally random behavior into sustained, goal-directed, and effective sequences of actions. The inner, mental states of purposefulness, desire, fright, etc., are parts of these sequences which can be felt "within the skin" but which, like the overt behavior, depend for their meaning and ap-parent goal-directedness on the shaping influences of past experience.

Skinner acknowledges that inner states of hunger, thirst, affection, and fear occur in the organism and have an insistent power. Some of the motivated feelings, for example, emerge with deprivation, because they are tied to innate physiological mechanisms; such feelings, however, become identified and incorporated into the goal-directed aspects of behavior in the immature organism because of their past successful relief by apt, reinforced actions. All aspects of behavior—its peculiarly teleological quality, its goal-direction, its associations with inner states of mind, its capacity for sequential complexity —can be derived by behaviorism from this appreciation of the interactions at the interface between the organism and the environment which is encapsulated in the phrase "past experience."

This is more than just a plausible proposal. The shaping of behavior can be demonstrated. Behaviorism forms the conceptual and technological basis of an extensive enterprise in research and has provided fresh insight into some psychiatric disorders. As an example, it proposes that some phobic conditions develop as aberrations of avoidance behavior, which normally serves to remove the individual from danger. Previously, such conditions had often proven refractory to both the insights of psychotherapy and the biological changes of drug treatments. The view that phobias were abnormally sustained, condi-tioned emotional responses that could be reshaped by "extinction" brought a new method of treatment with demonstrable success. It was also a vigorous challenge to the view that every symptom is a disguised manifestation of latent and unconscious motives and drives. The relief of these symptoms was not followed by the appearance of others, as that view would logically propose.

Yet the difficulties with behaviorism are also evident. Behaviorism promises more than it has delivered, as do most encompassing positions. The species generalizations from rats and pigeons to man and the environmental generaliza-tions from Skinner boxes to the world cannot be justified. For example, the attempt to explain language in behavioral terms that would ignore the intentionality and creativeness of human thinking and communication has been successfully refuted[150]. Taken to an extreme, behaviorism denies meaning to thought and freedom to choice.

Behavior is a domain special to psychiatry. The judgments within this domain are problematic in themselves and in what they are attempting to encompass. Explanations take from many sources, and although we must encourage the search for clear risk factors in problematic behaviors, in doing so we inevitably invoke concepts like choice, will, and meaning, which make the individual not only accountable for some part of his actions but also accessible to understanding and guidance that may modify attitudes crucial to his behavioral choices.

This viewpoint is central to our reasoning about behavior, in the clinic as well as in our daily lives. Human beings develop attitudes and intentions that are the most accessible causes of their behavior and that give a vitally satisfactory response to questions like, Why is this young woman not eating? The answer, Because she fears she may become too fat, begins an investigation into the meaning of the behavior which reveals the person as an empathically comprehensible subject, not just an object at the mercy of the forces that impinge on her.

To appreciate these issues we have to consider, in its most fundamental presentation, that perspective for individuals which seeks to discover the functions and meanings that underlie mental events and behaviors.

V

THE CONCEPT OF
THE LIFE STORY

18

The Individual:
A Consideration of the Self &
Its Relationship to
Life-Story Reasoning

In the preceding chapters we have tried to demonstrate that diseases, dimensions, and behaviors are observable regularities in human mental life and its disorders. We have focused on the conceptual characteristics and methodological rules that make these regularities comprehensible and have defined their utilization in descriptions of patients and research.

These regularities and their identification in mental distress and behavioral disorder are expressions of a search for forms. This method of employing the power of natural science within the area of disturbed behavior is not biological psychiatry, but it is empirical work, and it ultimately depends on our capacity to make observations of a reliable kind from studies of numerous patients and to propose hypotheses that can be challenged by further publicly verifiable observations. It is a growing part of psychiatry and links the field to other sciences by viewing man as an object within the forces of nature and as a subject/agent with certain predispositions and vulnerabilities to forces in society.

And yet, when we meet a patient, our knowledge of diseases, attributes, and motivated behaviors does not enable us to know him as a person. His individuality, expressed in opinions and choices, moods and whims, successes and failures, remains to confront our understanding of him and demands still another perspective.

If the brain-mind disjunction troubles psychiatry, in some contemporary behavioral sciences, *mind* is missing. Considerable information is available on brain correlates to behavior and on social forces and their influences on behavior, but with the sole exception of phenomenology (an operationally legitimated means of investigating the contents of the conscious mind), much of the individual's mental life and its implications for his behavior are ignored by scientists and left to practitioners to work out as best they can.

Because "mindless" but empirically sound psychiatry is often weak when faced with the individual and his options, it is hardly surprising that it holds little appeal for many practitioners. What they seek is something that will give them a sense of the meaningfulness, logic, and purpose behind the responses and behavior of their patients. Practitioners will thus accept a suggestion that enhances their persuasive power in a particular situation or a whole philosophy if it helps them to place the patient in a new perspective. They will accept much if it makes their daily round with patients one in which they can sense some meaning and act with purpose and authority. They will take truth if they can find it but will otherwise settle for what seems sensible until truth comes along.

Even after we have utilized the categorical distinctions of disease and its impairment, of the dimensional characteristics and their evoked vulnerabilities, and of the motivated behaviors and their effects on perception, choice, and learning we will still not have captured the individual and his intentions. *These* are the final arbiters of what can and will happen both to himself and to others. Why does *he* feel as he does, why does *he* think as he does, and why does *he* do what he does in a unique way, even though faced with situations similar to those that others face? These are the daily questions psychiatrists ask. Yet how can we have any systematic approach to such individual matters?

It may appear that there are only two alternatives: either to embrace science and reject the vagaries of individual issues, or to find a meaningful view that is comprehensive and submerge the objections to it, from scientists and others, by denying their legitimacy in empathically obvious situations. What one chooses and why are questions about physicians as intriguing as any to be found at the bedside. The choice illustrates that the issues here are far from simply clinical matters; they relate to our own personalities, educations, opinions, and ideologies. We think it possible to transcend these alternative positions by comprehending what is being attempted in understanding an individual. We can make such methods and the knowledge of individuals they bring part of our professional capacity without overextending their authority.

What, then, is individuality? What are the features of mental life which we are struggling to understand? What is the method that almost naturally is taken up to illuminate these issues? By individuality we mean the self, the sense of the person as the director or pilot of his life plan rather than as a reflexive or passive transmitter of bodily mechanisms, psychological predispositions, and life events. By the features of mental life here we mean the intentions of the self and their consequences in relation to other intentions, emotions, and behavior. By the illuminating method we mean the story technique used to render empathically plausible the connections between the life events, the self's intentions, and their consequences. The story told can be the briefest situational vignette or a full biographical history, but as a story its meanings and messages are those not only of the subject but also of the author. To comprehend this technique, therefore, we must appreciate the views and purposes of the author in constructing the story; by knowing, for example, that he emphasizes some things and ignores others. We use all of these interrelated concepts to see human behavior as expressing the functions of a person who can be understood from within a life story by our own natural capacities to empathize, to reexperience, and to build an imaginative reconstruction.

The Self or Subject/Agent

We mentioned before that the very sense of a self, an ego—a *me*—is the ultimate brain-mind problem. How a collection of organ systems can generate an expression not only of perception and feeling but also of independent control and direction of the mechanisms themselves is unknown. Although it may prove as illusory as the flat earth idea, so far we are left with the observation that everyone conceives of himself in this way, as directing to some extent his bodily mechanisms to purposes that he has "in mind." Similarly, an individual can often sense that he is not completely in control, as when he is impeded by symptoms of disease or coerced by the insistence of his motivated behaviors.

An excellent description of the concept of the self was given by William James, who tied it to the stream of consciousness and thought in which the memories, objects of perception, emotional tones, and life plans merge[151]. Freud also developed an elaborate set of functions that he tied to his concept of the ego, a self-like idea.

It is not our purpose to present differing conceptions of the self, however, so much as it is to recognize that perspective of clinical practice which depends on the sense that directing selves are in action. Any view that fails to take the self into account must seem impaired and limited. Yet what does it do for our reasoning?

First, it forces the *why* question upon us. That is, Why did he behave, respond, or react in that fashion rather than another? The *why* question (in contrast to the *how* or *how did it happen* questions) can only be answered from the reasons of a self, a subject/agent, somebody capable of making a plan, facing a decision, and choosing.

Second, it illuminates the self's existence in a world of choices, on which depend the achievements and the ultimate happiness and well-being of the self.

Third, the self is reflexive, as the term subject/agent implies. Even though limited by the tools at its disposal and the circumstances within which it must choose, the self can appreciate its own role in the outcome achieved. As such, it is the self and only the self that psychotherapy addresses. Psychotherapy aims to enable the self to be a more effective director of the life plan by enlarging its skills, altering its goals, or reflecting on its intentions. The reflexive capacity of the self is not limitless, however. Sometimes patients report that they have little or no understanding of the reasons for their thoughts and behaviors. This phenomenon had led to the proposal of a continuum of self-awareness described in terms of a conscious-unconscious dimension. In the process of psychotherapy it is essential to consider the possibility of unconscious mechanisms while avoiding their invocation to explain all mysteries.

Fourth, the self can be described in a number of ways. It can be viewed as a structure, as in Freud's tripartite id, ego, and superego; it can be presented as a series of roles, as in the transactionalist parent, adult, and child; or it can be seen as having developmental duties such as separation-individuation. In this way, differing approaches to intervention with the self can be proposed. But fundamentally these descriptions give meaningful names and roles to the self and are to be judged as useful metaphors if they open the self to the psychotherapist and to his attempt to see into the elements of its life plan.

The self is sometimes described as the agent of the life plan and at other times as the product of that life plan. Though these distinctions often become entangled, as they do in Freud's concept of the superego, it is usually possible to keep the empirical phenomenon of the self clear and separate from the functional roles given it by theorists.

Ids, egos, and superegos do not exist as forms of the self but as metaphors for some self-functions. They are popular devices for telling a particular kind of life story, and they assume certain things about man's "basic nature." In the clinical realm, however, they will eventually be used only by those who find them helpful and they will be neglected by those who find other ways to address the needs of the psychotherapeutic interaction.

These needs are, first, to have an illuminating conception of the self as an entity and, second, to have a means of expressing that conception which will prove acceptable and persuasive, either to the self in treatment or to the community of onlookers who support the therapeutic activities and judge the results. Fundamentally, to be effective with individual patients we need a psychiatry that utilizes the concept of a self in action regardless of what terms we employ for it and what functions we give it in the life story.

Intentions and Consequences

To ask the *why* question of mental life and its disorders assumes more than the sense of an agent in action. It assumes that at some level behavior is intentional, that it comes about as the result of such things as purposes, wishes, construals, and plans of the agent and that if these intentions were known, the behavior and the other responses of the self would then make sense. To say a response is meaningful is at the simplest level to say that it is connected to something else. That something can be a thought, a point of view, or a feeling. Through them, life circumstances can provoke behaviors and emotional reactions in the person.

In considering the intentions of the self we wish to include more than mental capacities such as intelligence. We also do not mean only issues of temperament that tend to dispose individuals to construe things in one way or another. Nor do we have in mind those aspects that derive from the motivated behaviors alone. These observable regularities certainly predispose and delimit the intentional aspects of the person, but despite all of them there are still unpredictable thoughts and feelings that are unique to the person and to his circumstances and that must be elucidated by some inquiry if his particular difficulties and behaviors are to be understood.

Many of these thoughts and feelings are easily determined by asking the person about them. He can tell about his aims and ambitions in his occupation, his views about significant people in his family, his values and their implications for his actions. It is often possible to discern a network of interrelated attitudes that constitute a self of particular inclinations. Knowledge of this network permits an accurate prediction of some responses and attitudes. A sense of how a person construes other people can be gleaned from so-called liberal and conservative stances, for example, which are expressed in voting records, party affiliations, and responses to particular appeals [152].

Thus, the sense of the role of the intentional in behavior is an everyday assumption that can be supported by empirical observations. In the clinic the intentional background to the patient's responses and behaviors must be explored if the aim is to appreciate the connections between his experiences and his difficulties. Basically, we want to know the intentions that help us comprehend this person.

A fundamental conception tied to this approach is that there are consequences to certain intentions that may be unwanted, unsought, and distressing but that are almost inevitable. Much of psychotherapy demonstrates how unintended consequences emerge from intentional actions. One can of course argue that all consequences are at some level, either conscious or unconscious, intended. The story of meaning can always be written in that way.

What we want to emphasize, however, is that many outcomes, including quite distressing ones, are the unwanted but predictable consequences of intentions accessible to consciousness. There are ways of construing oneself and others that make one vulnerable to losing friendships, to being exploited, to feeling disappointed, angry, or ineffective. Techniques for exploring these linkages between the intentional construals and the unintended consequences have stimulated interest and support for such therapies as Kelly's personal construct analysis[153] and Beck's cognitive approach[154].

Intentions are, however, limitless in their variety, as are the many consequences that can arise from them. One result of this variety is our almost irresistible urge to reduce the number of intentions to a basic few. By this reduction we retain the power of the meaningful connection of intentions to consequences and in fact enhance it by proposing that the conscious profusion of intentions is simply the distorted reflection of a few powerful and universal intentions such as those of sexuality or aggressiveness. When there is no way that such a proposal can be refuted, and when the intentions given this authority are plausible candidates for a dominating role (especially if unconscious mechanisms are invoked), it is easy to see how the proposal can succeed.

Yet much good psychiatry can be practiced utilizing complicated intentional contexts behind behaviors. The many possible intentions, for example, that link the behavior of hysteria to the sick role and to abnormal attitudes about illness have provided insights into individuals as well as concepts that can be empirically studied[155]. The capacity for this perspective to reveal issues of both form and function is also seen in bereavement and the process of grieving. Here, the emotion cannot be appreciated without some knowledge of the self and its commitments, but the state of grief is so regular in its manifestations that it can easily be recognized as a form of mental experience and can thus provide a focus for empirical as well as empathic study.

Life-Story Reasoning

If the self, its intentions, and their consequences are the ingredients of a meaningful psychiatry, the method we are here calling life-story reasoning is what gives them the power of conviction—the sense of knowing that is both illuminating and irresistible—and ties them together as dynamic functions with reflexive actions. For it is as stories that all of these issues are originally formulated, and it is through stories that the ideas are encountered, judged, and sustained.

It is true that occasionally someone develops a hypothesis from a story and tests it through the empirical-deductive method to find how good a generalization it is. But this is rare and seldom a source of persuasion for the meaningful approach. Here, the story and its interpretation of the self, its intentions, and their consequences are the driving force.

Every person is a story. There are as many stories as there are lives and there are many stories within each life. The story that is needed is the one that illuminates the clinical issue at hand. This can be an obvious story; when it is, there is usually immediate confirmation and support from the patient and from others. Occasionally the appropriate story is hard to find; then there is conflict, argument, and dissension.

The art of telling the best story for a particular patient depends on a capacity for imaginative reconstruction of his life circumstances, a faculty richly developed in Sigmund Freud and expressed in paradigmatic stories of psychoanalysis such as those of Anna O., Dora, and Little Hans. Such a skill can be developed, improved with practice, and helped by supervision from experienced psychotherapists. What is sought is what can fit, illuminate, and be accepted in sustaining the interaction of patient and therapist. In this regard, plausibility may be at least as important as historical truth.

Although life stories embody the analysis of function both for particular clinical problems and for the general theories that can arise from this method, it is difficult to define the source of the story's authority. It is important to appreciate that such stories are neither data from which theories emerge nor indisputable facts.

Stories are not data, the raw material or elemental observations that form the basis for an inference or an interpretation, but are themselves interpretations that relate, in narrative form, events from the patient's past to his current symptoms in a fashion that makes the development of those symptoms seem explained.

Stories are not facts, although they may be partially constituted from them. The story is a construction about the linkages between events, a compound of facts and presumptions, some of which are reported by the patient and others assumed by the author.

Many of the events of the story do not have an existence that can be demonstrated independently of the knowing subject and the story's author. A crucial event in the development of psychoanalysis was Freud's shift from the assumption of the historical fact of childhood seduction in the genesis of hysteria to the conception of the presence of an unconscious wish that provided the source for both the false recollections he first encountered and the hysterical symptoms he sought to understand. From Freud we have come to accept as appropriate events for a clinical story the distorted wishes and defensive reactions to conflicts that exist only as reported by the patient and as intepreted by the therapist. But if life stories are neither data nor facts, what are they?

Life stories are symbols. They impart a sense of knowing that persuades through imagery and fellow-feeling. They progress not on a single level of analysis but on multiple ones simultaneously, encompassing considerations such as diseases, traits, and motivations along with theoretical assumptions and the individual events of the life in question. All these considerations are condensed by the story into a unity that is at once a unique explanation for a particular clinical occasion and a symbol that can be made to represent either the patient himself or an aspect of human nature.

The symbolic story has the power to express what cold logic struggles with: the reality of inner conflicts, incompatibilities, and tensions. It describes these issues in a way that makes them vivid and that places them in an appropriate perspective. The very composition of the symbolic story moves these issues from the twilight of the unobjectified into the clarity of consciousness for both the subject of the story and its author. As this process is completed the story can begin to serve as the starting point for new intentions and for a new life plan.

The story is composed in the relationship between patient and physician. It derives most of its power to produce change in the patient from this context. The story may appear to be concerned only with the transmission of information (for example, a means for the doctor to point out a pathogenic effect of a particular childhood experience, or to explain the "true" source of the patient's attitudes). Actually it is a means of persuasion ("try to see yourself in this way and act accordingly"). The story often has a more relational than informational purpose. It mediates a common vision for the patient and the physician, and by altering the patient's understandings, intentions, and other relationships, it suggests ways of confronting the future. The situation it *produces* as much as the particular information it conveys gives the story its point [26].

The story's power, then, is the power of all symbols to persuade, to inspire, and sometimes to seduce, an authority that may place it beyond the reach of logic and the challenge of refutation. This authority inspires some of the confidence of those who choose, and much of the concern of those who question, this way of reasoning about patients.

What stories, what networks of meaningful connections, tend to be told? Stories usually take advantage of themes that can enhance their plausibility. Thus the concept of development, so crucial to our understanding of motivated behaviors and so obvious an aspect of human life, can be employed in the simplest vignettes of maternal separation and childhood distress, of pubescent shyness and sibling rivalry. More elaborate and more problematic stories derived from the same source might link a young woman's anorexia nervosa to an expression of her unwillingness to grow up, to the challenge of sexuality, to her rejection of her mother's care, or to her primitive views on conception. It is from the stories with developmental themes that we derive such generalizations about human nature as penis envy, castration anxiety, separation-individuation, and the mid-life crisis.

A characteristic of story-based ideas is that what they propose tends to be considered a universal feature of mankind though the evidence for that claim is distilled from the stories of a few selected individuals. These generalizations thus resemble proverbs and maxims to be applied in a clinical narrative more than they do hypotheses or laws that can be used to account for thoughts, emotions, and behaviors with defined confidence limits. Examples of such maxims are Breuer and Freud's statement, *"Hysterics suffer mainly from reminiscences"* [156] and Sullivan's dictum, *"The obsessional neurotic has never had the satisfaction of outstanding success in interpersonal relations"* [157].

These maxims both derive from and help to illuminate the life stories of patients. Not only are the individual and his circumstances more complex than any maxim can encompass, but in addition, an awkward feature of maxims is that their opposites are equally true. Even the most apt one needs the life story itself to draw all of the clinical data together into a dynamic, meaningful, and particular whole.

As mentioned above, the meaning is actually constructed and advocated by some author of the story. He will build it not only from the patient's reports but also from his own experiences and opinions. The patient may accept it or reject it for many reasons, but never because he can prove or disprove it.

It is in the effort to produce from stories a more complete view of mankind that this method tends to develop a philosophical schema, a "metapsychology," as Freud called it, in which the generalizations about the self and its intentionality are employed to understand human nature, history, and civilization. In a metapsychology some fundamental assumption directs the stories and their linkages. For Freud, various ideas are claimed as central to his philosophical stance. Thus, some of his students find that Freud's views on psychic determinism and the unconscious are his major contributions, whereas others believe that it is his concept of transference in relationships.

For us, the central Freudian concept that holds throughout his work, both in his case studies and in his elaborated theories, is the idea that the manifest contents of consciousness, including the acknowledged intentions of the self, are distorted elements derived from an unconscious and latent realm. In this realm primitive motivated drives are held back from consciousness by the repressive, defensive forces of the ego. The process of transforming unconscious motives into conscious acts is the essence of the Freudian story.

Every story for Freud and his followers, even if they disagree about which drives are paramount, is an exercise in hermeneutics: a reading of the books of consciousness and behavior for their hidden meanings, an unveiling of the purposes and functions of the self. This reading is done by someone who knows what is to be found and who makes of each clinical encounter a reiteration rather than a test of the vision. That which is known is rediscovered in a new story to encourage the knower in his opinion and to enhance his commitment to what was assumed at the start.

Freud's achievement is to make us think in terms of hidden meanings and to appreciate the role of the unobjectified and unacknowledged in certain situations. Yet we must resist the temptation to think in these terms always and so to neglect simpler explanations of action and thought.

We are thus returned to our beginnings, finding here within the self and its intentionality the full expression of a psychiatry of function. How shall we make most use of it? Can we control this method and make its products our own?

19

The Strengths, Limitations, & Recognition of The Life-Story Method of Reasoning

B efore we can consider the most obvious strengths and limitations of the story method, there is an aspect expressed in its practical outcome—psychotherapy—that should be made explicit because it is often lost in the medical overtones of the term *therapy*. It is a distinction in the way this method conceptualizes its tasks in relation to the patient, his present state, and his future.

The concept of disease presumes the presence of a pathological process in action, a process that causes symptoms in the present and that constrains the patient's future in predictable ways. The best treatment will interrupt that process and its success will be unambiguous: relief of current symptoms and freedom from their return as products of the disease in question.

Psychotherapy and the story method that informs it begin with present complaints but consider them and any prediction of the future primarily in terms of the patient's past. Present and future derive not from the effects of some ongoing process but from the poorly conceived or conflicted decisions of the self, which bring about unintended and unfortunate consequences.

Whereas in the disease construct it is the pathological process that evokes a crippled future, the story attempts to show that it is the self's intentions that lead to the consequences seen in the present and expected in the future. Psychotherapy is not an effort to interrupt a process of a specified character that has a predictable course. It is an effort to help a person choose to live more successfully in the present and to confront any future more effectively. Its aim is a person perfected, in the sense of an understanding more fully developed, rather than a disease cured or an injury healed.

This is a shift of premise with many implications, two of which need emphasis. First, the life-story method is suited for its aim because it provides the patient and the therapist with a dramatized and memorable way of discovering the interaction of events and intentions which led to the present. It also provides an illumination and inspiration that can facilitate the mutual effort to discern more effective approaches to the future. Second, the criteria for success in this enterprise are elusive and value laden because they rest, not on the demonstration of a future free from the effects of a specific process, but on the reports of satisfaction by the self and on abstract comparisons of paths of life to be chosen or rejected.

Because psychotherapy and the life-story technique are based on satisfaction and intentional choices, they are brought into a dialogue, if not a confrontation, with "ultimate concerns." It goes beyond our purpose in this short book to mediate in that dialogue, but it remains a crucial though seldom-discussed aspect of this domain. The "ultimate concerns" promulgated by a story-based psychiatry can and should be compared with those from other encompassing views about mankind such as the philosophical and the religious. Although this comparison invokes a domain of challenge and accountability unfamiliar to and usually unsought by physicians, it remains true that values here are often propagated by insinuation rather than by direct argument. In discussions about the best way to live a life, psychiatrists do not, simply by virtue of their professional educations, have the final jurisdiction.

The Strengths of the Story Method

It is easy to appreciate the power of the life-story method, a power that links the self, its intentions, and their consequences. To see these playing out their themes in a narrative is to see them in the most natural way.

In a story anything can be employed to make the narrative meaningful. The elements of mental life that we have considered "forms" can be used, as when the subject's distinctive temperament, his impairments of cognition, or his motivations add clinical comprehensiveness to the story. These phenomena become part of the characterization of the self and help to clarify aspects of its intentions. This is sometimes viewed as "having it both ways"; that is, being scientific and empathic. But it is crucial to understand that a scientific method is not being combined with a story. The story will remain dominant if the purpose is to understand this individual and his particular circumstance, regardless of its ingredients and their sources.

A story is a vivid way to capture a part of reality—reality as it is experienced and lived. No other method can give this sense of immediacy. In addition, the story provides for the sense of complexity in mental life. Because stories are endless in their variety, they are immune to the criticism that "things are more complicated than any science can imagine." If such a point is made about a particular story, it is answered with a more detailed narrative that further develops the various themes in the story's plot.

The story is the best way to enhance our empathic appreciation of the patient, because it views him as a fellow being caught up in life's processes. Our ability to help him and even our desire to help him depend to a considerable degree on this appreciation. No alien object is the protagonist of the story; he is always a person like us, with hopes, fears, and intentions. We can help only if we understand.

The story has particular advantages for a patient in distress. It produces a sense of relief and a hope of being understood and appreciated by someone else, particularly when that someone proposes a view that brings order out of chaos. This relief not only diminishes the patient's pessimistic state but also persuades him to trust and rely upon the psychiatrist, whose stature is enhanced by the insights he reveals in supplying an apt explanatory story. The story thus works at many levels, and binds together its subject and its author in an enterprise of changing the future.

The story usually fits the times, a characteristic that can account for both its contemporary persuasiveness and its eventual replacement. Some of the power of the Freudian vision rests on its mixture of classical mechanics, Romantic imagery, and a secular world-view familiar to the liberal intellectual community. That Jungian analytic psychology was less popular originally may be attributable in part to its unfashionable emphasis on the mystical and the supernatural; yet now there are many people who find insights about their lives in the Jungian conception.

It is the story method that is being proposed when physicians claim the importance of appreciating the "whole" patient or "holistic" medicine. It is clearly an improvement in our understanding of any individual to see not only his diseased state but also his sense that he is in the midst of a crucial situation in his life. Holistic medicine is fundamentally the combination of knowledge of the patient's disease and his personal story. By giving the patient time to tell his story as he sees it, and through an appreciation of other stories like it, the physician can understand and assist the patient with his emotional and behavioral reactions. Listening is only the first step, but it is essential in transforming the clinical problem from the treatment of diseases to the healing of individuals.

The Limitations of the Story Method

The limitations of the story method are largely the obverse of its strengths. First, the patient's story is appreciated and written by authors who see and hear from the patient some things and not others. The story method brings out professional conflicts in a way other methods do not. It is impossible to judge the story without judging the storyteller. This phenomenon may have contributed to the remarkable animosities between Freud, Jung, and Adler. In fact, not only is it often felt that what story you find in your patients determines what type of practitioner you are, but it can sometimes also seem that opting for the story method can mark you as a good psychiatrist in some places and a bad psychiatrist in others.

Next, psychiatrists are not immune to the herd instinct that can bedevil all storytellers. They may see in their patients what others tell them they should see. And because a harmony with the spirit of the times may be as crucial for therapeutic purposes as it is for satisfying publishers and editors, psychiatrists, like journalists, may repeat a version of the same story on occasion after occasion.

Stories are encountered, written, and experienced. They are not refutable and are difficult even to challenge by the techniques of reliability and validity. The story is often crucial to the psychotherapeutic process, but whether the particular story is more important than the sense of caring and optimism in the practitioner (perhaps generated by his commitment to the story he tells) is difficult to know.

The story presents us with a dictum about the patient. It disrupts rational argument because criticism of its logic or complaints about its biases can be interpreted either as missing the point or as "resistance" on the part of the critic. Nonetheless, the story method is vulnerable to two potential errors: the choice of the story method rather than another category of explanation, and the choice of the wrong story from among the several in a person's life.

The erroneous choice of the story perspective for a patient with a disease does more than deprive him of the strengths of the disease method (specific treatment and prognosis); it burdens the clinical situation with the limitations of the story method without conferring its advantages.

The most obvious of these limitations is felt by members of the patient's family. The story, because of its power to create symbols, can transform relatives into passive figures or role players in the patient's life story, a transformation that renders them relatively impotent to contribute to the patient's recovery. They may sense a collusion of patient and therapist in an interpretation of all their actions and opinions. They often feel trapped by a set of conceptions about them that treats, by a kind of "looking-glass logic," each of their efforts as an expression of the same predetermined, story-designated role. The resentments and sense of ill-usage that this provokes injure the network of support that the patient with a disease needs to carry him through his illness and convalescence.

A similar set of problems is felt by family members if the wrong story is told. In these circumstances they are depicted as role players in an erroneous story but can produce no effective criticism of it.

Reasoning by the life-story method can evolve a set of premises that jeopardizes both the method's own foundation and elements of its utility. Out of the sense of inevitability tied to the narrative line in any individual life story can come the view that the accountable, deciding, and thus to some extent free and responsible, self is an illusion. Because the self *did* act in one way, it *had* to act in that way. The very phenomenon—the self—that psychiatrists who are alert to individuals have preserved from the determinants of biology, constitution, and disease is then abandoned for the opinion, derived from a series of meaningful connections, that the self always acts in response to some basic motivated drive but rationalizes its conduct as freely chosen by repressing knowledge of the conduct's "actual" source and "true" goal.

This theoretical position is not a necessary consequence of life-story reasoning, but it can arise from the method, and particularly from the force, of the narrative line. This force comes from combining a retrospective choice among life happenings with the tendency of empathy to turn possible connections between events and behavior into inevitable sequences.

A premise of determinism is, however, never demonstrated by retrospective observations, and we do not need to assume determinism when we say that we understand an individual from his life's story. We propose one sequence of meaningful connections and its outcome, but many others could be imagined and produced. In fact, if the premise of absolute determinism is accepted, psychotherapy must appear a futile endeavor. Psychotherapy ultimately depends on the capacity of the self to change, and at some level it must be free to do so.

The premise of determinism and the denial of freedom have far-reaching consequences for the interactions of psychiatry with other social institutions such as government. A democratic society is based on the assumption of human freedom and must provide settings that enhance it. A set of psychiatric premises, however kindly intended for patient care, that subverts that assumption for the governed is itself repressive and will disrupt the relationship of psychiatry with the community that supports it. Such unprovable and unnecessary premises, like all encompassing views that limit the self by proposing some "basic nature" of mankind, must have regrettable effects.

Despite its limitations, however, the life-story method's employment is essential and inevitable in psychiatric practice. It is a method of explanation that we must not only reason with but also reason about. It is often the life-story method that brings a meaningful encounter with our patients.

The standards by which a story is judged are identical to those employed in evaluating a historical interpretation. From recorded information about events, chronology, and people, history develops a view of their interaction that makes sense of them and fits them into current historical understanding. Similarly, from the events, responses, and intentions of a patient's life, psychiatrists build a story that explains the clinical outcome and encompasses the course of its development. The power of the story resides in its meaningful grasp of these issues within a narrative, but to be effective in therapy a story must be both simple enough to be memorable and complex enough to be comprehensive.

How the Story Is Recognized

The story method can be recognized most easily in any explanatory proposal that seems to rest on the life experience of some particular person. The Freudian stories of Anna O., Dora, and Schreber are typical examples. But any ascription of a mental phenomenon to a personal experience employs the story method; for example, in Freud's *Psychopathology of Everyday Life* he described how his own slips of the tongue and pen are explained by their relationships to his present concerns, offering a number of little vignettes that illuminate the meaning of some simple phenomena [158].

We can also recognize the story method even though no particular person is being discussed. Terms such as *roles, character, acting out,* or *stigma* imply a world of actors, protagonists, responsive subjects, and the events of a story.

Even the therapeutic encounter may be described in story terms. Psychoanalytic opinion that the transference relationship is the critical aspect of therapy may or may not be true, but it proposes a very special role for the therapist and an intriguing and bold conception of the situation. The therapist is not an adviser. Rather, he is thought to reveal the patient's intentions indirectly in a kind of "play within a play." His treatment rests not on his direction of the play but with his entrance into the drama of the patient's life story. A repetition of the patient's habitual story line with significant figures in his life is permitted to be replayed, and from the more neutral stance of the analyst it can be observed and gradually "worked through." The story is re-lived and life then replotted.

The story method often gets buried in the metatheory that the stories have engendered. In these circumstances the method may be difficult to identify, but there are ways to recognize it in its metatheory form. First, one should perhaps assume the presence of the story method when there is no effort to provide any limits to the opinions offered. From the certainty with which the theory is presented it might not seem that there are issues that could be misidentified or misinterpreted, though such doubts usually occur naturally in other methods of explanation.

Second, the story method is probably present when no enumeration of successes and failures, errors and corrections, is presented. An authority above such issues may seem compelling given the plausibility of the story or given assumptions about the professional skill of the author based on his position, responsibilities, acknowledged experience, or intellectual gifts.

Third, the story method is present when the generalizations are universal aspects of mankind and yet the observations behind those conclusions seem elusive or singular. "Castration anxiety," "inferiority complex," and "earth mother" are examples that may well be found in individual stories but that have also been proposed as universal human attributes.

Fourth, the story approach may be an essential, if unidentified, part of a mixture of methods constituting a theory. Again, "holistic" medicine usually assumes a story. Systems theorists occasionally describe their work as though they were sustaining a similar method of reasoning as they pass up the hierarchies of organization within the "biopsychosocial" approach to human beings. But while empirical methods are employed at some levels of the hierarchy, the story method appears in others. This crucial shift may affect the nature of conclusions and our confidence in them but it may not be noticed or commented upon.

Recapitulation: The Story Method and Reasoning in Psychiatry

Throughout this book we have been interested in what we know and how we know it, so it is appropriate here to make several general points about the story method. It is not an infallible key to man and his civilization. Rather, it is a method that is very vulnerable to the preconceptions of the author about these matters. It can be a most seductive way of proposing a world-view because it assumes the neutrality of the clinic even though it may not share it. An example of how far this can be carried is found in the language of Foucault's *Madness and Civilization:*

> At the end of the Middle Ages, leprosy disappeared from the Western world. In the margins of the community, at the gates of cities, there stretched wastelands which sickness had ceased to haunt but had left sterile and long uninhabitable. For centuries, these reaches would belong to the non-human. From the fourteenth to the seventeenth century, they would wait, soliciting with strange incantations a new incarnation of disease, another grimace of terror, renewed rites of purification and exclusion. . . .
> Leprosy disappeared, the leper vanished, or almost, from memory. . . .
> Often, in these same places, the formulas of exclusion would be repeated, strangely similar two or three centuries later. Poor vagabonds, criminals, and "deranged minds" would take the part played by the leper, and we shall see what salvation was expected from this exclusion, for them and for those who excluded them as well [159].

The story method does not provide new information about nature, but it can provide a way of describing how some of us experience the world. This is its most helpful and, indeed, its essential characteristic. We need to be aware of this fact in the clinic and to be prepared to defend the story method as a powerful technique for revealing and assisting in some way common human predicaments. If we hope to diminish the unintended consequences of intentional actions, we must be able to see the story behind the actor. If we want to treat the symptoms of disease, we must be able to see the organism behind the man. Both approaches begin as methods of reasoning.

VI

CONFLICTS
& CONCEPTS

20

The Need for Integration

The parable of the blind men each attempting to describe an elephant while palpating one of its several appendages has been used to depict the different schools of psychiatry, each of which emphasizes one approach and seems unaware of others. Such a metaphor captures the groping for an elusive central concept that is an aspect of most students' experiences in this field, but it errs in an important respect. In psychiatry there is no "elephant"; there are only appendages. There is no "unified field theory" from which we derive all the information necessary for the discipline.

A better metaphor might describe psychiatry as a fabric of distinct themes: a warp of constructs—disease categories, dimensions, behaviors, individual life stories—tied together by a woof of explanatory methods that we have entitled the approaches to explaining forms (answering *what* and *how* questions) and to explaining functions (answering the *why* question) (fig. 4). Each construct and explanatory method has its own set of premises, store of facts, and mode of progression, which are, to a degree remarkable in medicine, distinct from the others. But each must be woven into a comprehensive design in every clinical encounter. It is their separate but interlocking character that we have attempted to depict in the preceding chapters.

An important consequence of reasoning from distinct concepts is that category errors can be appreciated and avoided. From what we have written it should be clear, for example, that an approach to the study of dementia should follow a different course from an approach to the understanding of grief. To assess dementia as a reaction to life circumstances or to view grief as a disease would be to work with the wrong premises and constructs. Nonetheless, the explanatory methods of both form and function can be employed in each of these conditions, though in different ways to provide different information.

143

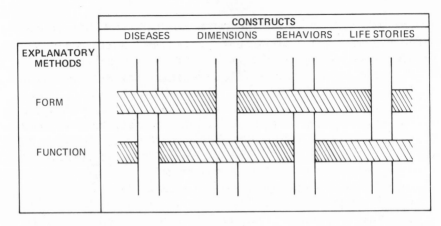

FIGURE 4

There are clear formal elements that distinguish dementia from grief. A form analysis would attempt to identify those elements and then to account for them in terms of brain pathology on the one hand and life events on the other. There are also functional aspects that emerge in each of these conditions. In dementia, aspects of personality, past experience, and current relationships play important roles in understanding the patient's emotional reactions to his impairment. In grief the meaning of loss to the individual, the type of person he is, the circumstances of the moment, and the nature of the supports available in the past and provided in the present are crucial to illuminate why he has reacted as he has.

Even if category errors are avoided, the crisscross of themes in psychiatry can bewilder the beginner. In a clinical or theoretical situation are we trying to describe a mental state, define a category of disease, explain a behavior, understand a troubled person, or all of these things simultaneously? If we emphasize scientific explanation for a group of patients with a disease today, does that mean we will deny empathic understanding to an individual in distress tomorrow? Where is progress to come in this discipline and how will we know it? These are questions that illustrate the complicated status of psychiatry as an intellectual enterprise.

In this book we have tried to show that each of the interlocking themes must be comprehended for itself. This is one way to avoid the discord and confusion that befalls the field when the application of one perspective or another is inappropriate.

And yet there are issues that will always remain problematic because of the fabriclike nature of the discipline and its lack of a "unified field theory." Thus, classificatory systems are often unsatisfactory in psychiatry no matter how well the issues of operationalism, reliability, and validity are addressed. A classificatory system, if it is any kind of "system" at all, must find some consistent perspective for its framework. The perspectives of psychiatry, however, are several, and no single classification can easily encompass them.

DSM-III is an advance over *DSM-II.* It argues for publicly accessible criteria in diagnosis and for categories that are strict and conceptually clear, and it incorporates empirical research about psychiatric conditions into classification. From this it can be appreciated that its strengths are most obvious in the categorical conditions such as the diseases and that it labors to cope with clinical situations in which the individual contributions from personality, life circumstance, and sociocultural situation intermingle.

Psychiatry may always find itself involved in battles, most often and most injuriously from partisans of one perspective who fail to give legitimacy to another. The recent claims of the "antipsychiatrists" are examples of this vulnerability in a discipline of multiple perspectives.

The "death of psychiatry" wing of this movement proposes that because the major disease categories will likely prove to have brain pathology, the care of patients with such illnesses will devolve to neurologists. And because a medical degree is not required to provide psychotherapy, patients with symptoms not caused by diseases will be treated by psychologists, social workers, nurses, and lay therapists. There will be nothing left for psychiatry to call its own and it will therefore wither away.

This syllogism succeeds only by defining psychiatry as a discipline that ignores the diseases tied to the brain (for example, dementia, delirium, and some forms of mental retardation) and that approaches the issues of personality disorder, behavior, and the self solely in terms of therapy (and not in terms of differential diagnosis, prognosis, and research). A psychiatry that sees itself as a discipline of several distinct constructs and methods of explanation, all of which interrelate in an attempt to help patients with abnormal mental states and behaviors, has been overlooked by this view. Such a psychiatry will only grow and prosper with further knowledge of the brain and from collaboration with other disciplines.

Similarly, *The Myth of Mental Illness* [160] argues from a category error. One can agree with Thomas Szasz that hysteria is not a disease and that those who, like Charcot, considered it as such were wrong. But that does not imply that other conditions treated by psychiatrists should not be construed as diseases before a pathology has been found for them. The disease construct is a means of reasoning about clinical data in an attempt to explain them. It is no more or less a myth than any construct; it is a premise that may or may not be validated for any given condition. The legitimacy of psychiatry as a medical specialty, however, does not rest only on the discovery of diseases, because they are not the only things that disturb mental life and behavior. Some psychiatric conditions *are* diseases in all that the term implies, but others are not, belonging instead to other constructs within the field, such as reactions, behaviors, and life stories.

Psychiatry's critics often cite forensic issues and condemn psychiatrists who confine patients involuntarily or who offer reasons to reduce the punishment of certain individuals who break the law. These arguments tend to assume that all psychiatric patients are fundamentally the same and differ from normal only in degree. Therefore, in fairness, the law should not treat them differently from other people: none should be placed in a hospital without his agreement and all should suffer the full penalty of the law for their behaviors.

A response to this view is that psychiatric patients are far from a homogeneous group. Some are individuals damaged as organisms and constrained in their thoughts, behaviors, and choices by the stereotypy and progression of disease. It is the task of psychiatry to recognize and distinguish them from other people whose emotional responses differ in degree but not in kind from those of the general population.

Society can decide how it will apply these distinctions in its law. It already does so with certain issues in which seemingly similar behaviors rest on different causes. A person can write a will that deprives his heirs of his estate. If he does so because he is angry or spiteful the law still sanctions his action. If, however, he does so under the delusional belief that his heirs are impostors, the law rejects the will and denies him "testamentary capacity." Thus, laws can be made which recognize the fact that under the influence of certain conditions people may not "know" what they are doing. Similar reasoning can justify the use of hospital commitment and the "insanity plea."

"Antipsychiatry," however, is a sideshow with allure primarily for the inexperienced. It is a form of intellectual kitsch marked by sensationalism and sentimentality. It evaporates as an issue for most students after they encounter the reality of mental illness.

There is, however, a major problem that derives from psychiatry's character as a discipline of interwoven constructs and explanations. This problem is tied to therapeutics and takes the form of a contradiction of equally true principles. Treatment requires confidence for success, but an overly confident therapeutics is an obstacle to progress.

Great confidence is needed to plan and carry out a course of psychotherapy that would alter the attitudes and directions of a self in action. This confidence may be fostered by associations of therapists in which they are able to develop a common language, conceptual grasp, and treatment approach. Confidence is sustained by mutual support and the recounting of success, but there is usually little questioning of first principles or advocacy for research to test the efficacy of treatments.

The opposition to the therapeutic institute comes from a desire for publicly demonstrable progress. Thus, the inquiry of empiricism often brings a rebuke to the therapist's assumptions and aspirations because it properly claims that only research will produce a future psychiatry with justified confidence in its therapeutics. A concern for reliability and validity can therefore seem to disparage efforts offered for the care of individuals. But erroneous enthusiasms of any kind can lead to mistreatment.

It remains our point that to know these problems is to be armed against them. One need not be swept into a community of therapists to appreciate the confidence such communities give in an uncertain enterprise or to be wary of the intellectual authoritarianism they can promote. One can also join in research without losing an appreciation for the art of helping a troubled person.

By emphasizing the most practical source of conflict in psychiatry—the need for both therapeutic confidence and investigative challenge—we do not mean to minimize the more abstract sources of contention. They also derive from the fabriclike character of this field and, like the practical sources of contention, these abstract tensions array themselves in dialectical pairs: form and function, object/organism and subject/agent, a disease cured and a person perfected. They all have champions and challengers pointing to the good to be found on one side and the danger on the other. Such conflicts are inherent to our discipline, but their elucidation shows that neither bad motives, bad physicians, nor bad patients are at fault. At least one root of the problem is a confusion over what we know and how we know it.

We have focused primarily on the constructs, or perspectives, that attempt to make the observations of patients comprehensible. We believe that the understanding of perspectives is difficult for beginners and is the source of much of the contention in psychiatry. If the approach to perspectives is grasped then the linkages of observations will become obvious, as will the nature of disagreements and some of the means to resolve them.

We see four major perspectives that attempt to make sense of the clinical presentations of patients. These are diseases, dimensions, behaviors, and life stories. Although they can often coexist in a clinical situation, it should now be clear that each depends on different domains for its acceptance: disease, for example, on the demonstration of pathology within a bodily part; dimensions, on discriminable distributions and the prediction of future performance from positions on the dimensional axis.

A psychiatrist can choose any perspective or construe new ones to explain a patient's symptoms. He can call on the disease concept if he thinks that biological information, present or future, will discern the bodily part affected, or he can propose the life story if he thinks it will illuminate the relationships between events and emotional responses.

He is free to choose or to change his perspective, but the choice, once made, always presents him with a set of demands that extend from the particular patient to an understanding of the choice itself. A change of perspective is not a release from responsibility; it is only a shift to a different set of demands. One understands a perspective and can be accountable for its choice when one can define the relevant domains from which its validation should emerge and can describe the explanatory themes that those domains support.

By insisting on this kind of reasoning, psychiatry can encourage ingenuity and creative insight without fearing a future of confusion, enthusiasms, and acrimony. One can "let a hundred flowers blossom, a hundred schools of thought contend" if the ground from which the flowers emerge is well surveyed and constantly under cultivation.

References

1. Murphy EA: Skepsis, Dogma, and Belief: Uses and Abuses in Medicine. Baltimore, Johns Hopkins University Press, 1981, p 14

2. Bridgman PW: The Logic of Modern Physics. New York, Macmillan, 1928, p 5

3. Fiegl H: Operationism and scientific method. Psychol Rev 52:250-259, 1945

4. Jaspers K: General Psychopathology. Chicago, University of Chicago Press, 1963, p 55

5. Bridgman PW: The Way Things Are. Cambridge, Harvard University Press, 1959, p 220

6. Leff JP: Psychiatrists' versus patients' concepts of unpleasant emotions. Br J Psychiatry 133:306-313, 1978

7. Romano J, Engel GL: Delirium: I. Electroencephalographic data. Arch Neurology and Psychiatry 51:356-377, 1944

8. Kelly DHW: Measurement of anxiety by forearm blood flow. Br J Psychiatry 112:789-798, 1966

9. Kreitman N, Sainsbury P, Morrissey J, et al: The reliability of psychiatric assessment: An analysis. J Ment Sci 107:887-908, 1961

10. Luria R, McHugh PR: The reliability and clinical utility of the Present State Examination. Arch Gen Psychiatry 30:866-871, 1974

11. Andreasen NC: Affective flattening and the criteria for schizophrenia. Am J Psychiatry 136:944-947, 1979

12. Rutter M, Cox A: Psychiatric interviewing techniques: I. Methods and measures. Br J Psychiatry 138:273-282, 1981

13. Kuhn TS: The Structure of Scientific Revolutions (ed 2). Chicago, University of Chicago Press, 1970

14. Zubin J: Classification of behavior disorders, in Farnsworth, PR (ed): Annual Review of Psychology (vol 19), Palo Alto, Annual Reviews, 1967, pp 373-406

15. Peroutka SJ, Snyder SH: Relationship of neuroleptic drug effects at brain dopamine, serotonin, α-adrenergic, and histamine receptors to clinical potency. Am J Psychiatry 137:1518-1522, 1980

16. Snyder SH: Amphetamine psychosis: A "model" schizophrenia mediated by catecholamines. Am J Psychiatry 130:61-67, 1973

17. Swank RL: Combat exhaustion: A description and statistical analysis of causes, symptoms and signs. J Nerv Ment Dis 109:475-508, 1949

18. Brown GW, Harris T: Social Origins of Depression: A Study of Psychiatric Disorder in Women. New York, Free Press, 1978

19. Mischel T: Psychological explanations and their vicissitudes, in Arnold WJ (ed): Nebraska Symposium on Motivation, 1975 (vol 23). Lincoln, University of Nebraska Press, pp 133-204

20. Smith GP: Satiety and the problem of motivation, in Pfaff DW (ed): The Physiological Mechanisms of Motivation. New York, Springer-Verlag, 1982, pp 133-143

21. Freud S: Five lectures on psychoanalysis, in Strachey J (ed): The Standard Edition of the Complete Psychological Works of Sigmund Freud (vol 11). London, Hogarth Press, 1957, pp 37-38

22. Freud S: Five lectures on psychoanalysis, in Strachey J (ed): The Standard Edition of the Complete Psychological Works of Sigmund Freud (vol 11). London, Hogarth Press, 1957, p 49

23. Ricoeur P: Freud and Philosophy. New Haven, Yale University Press, 1970, p 4

24. Jaspers K: General Psychopathology. Chicago, University of Chicago Press, 1963, pp 805-822

25. Wolberg LR: The Technique of Psychotherapy (ed 2). New York, Grune and Stratton, 1967, pp 375-398

26. Frank JD: Persuasion and Healing: A Comparative Study of Psychotherapy (rev ed). Baltimore, Johns Hopkins University Press, 1973, pp 166-199

27. Wing JK: Reasoning about Madness. Oxford, Oxford University Press, 1978, p 45

28. Allport GW: Personality: A Psychological Interpretation. New York, Henry Holt, 1937, p 22

29. Jaspers K: General Psychopathology. Chicago, University of Chicago Press, 1963, pp 301-303

30. Popper K: Conjectures and Refutations: The Growth of Scientific Knowledge. London, Routledge and Kegan Paul, 1963, pp 33-39

31. Habermas J: Knowledge and Human Interest. Boston, Beacon Press, 1971, pp 308-310

32. Edwards G, Gross MM: Alcohol dependence: provisional description of a clinical syndrome. Br Med J 1:1058-1061, 1976

33. Scadding JG: Diagnosis: The clinician and the computer. Lancet ii:877-882, 1967

34. Kendell RE: The concept of disease and its implications for psychiatry. Br J Psychiatry 127:305-315, 1975

35. Taylor F Kräupl: The medical model of the disease concept. Br J Psychiatry 128:588-594, 1976

36. Wing JK: Reasoning About Madness. Oxford, Oxford University Press, 1978, pp 21-42

37. Sydenham T: The Works of Thomas Sydenham, M.D. (vol 1). London, Sydenham Society, 1848, pp 13-17

38. Sigerist HE: The Great Doctors. New York, W W Norton, 1933, p 181

39. Taylor F Kräupl: Psychopathology (rev ed). Baltimore, Johns Hopkins University Press, 1979, p 5

40. Sigerist HE: The Great Doctors. New York, W W Norton, 1933, pp 233-234

41. Taylor F Kräupl: Psychopathology (rev ed). Baltimore, Johns Hopkins University Press, 1979, p 8

42. Sigerist HE: The Great Doctors. New York, W W Norton, 1933, pp 371-372

43. Blessed G, Tomlinson BE, Roth M: The association between quantitative measures of dementia and of degenerative changes in the cerebral grey matter of elderly subjects. Br J Psychiatry 114:797-811, 1968

44. Perry EK, Tomlinson BE, Blessed G, et al: Correlation of cholinergic abnormalities with senile plaques and mental test scores in senile dementia. Br Med J 2:1457-1459, 1978

45. Whitehouse PJ, Price DL, Clark AW, Coyle JT, DeLong MR: Alzheimer's disease: Evidence for selective loss of cholinergic neurons in the nucleus basalis. Ann Neurol 10:122-126, 1981

46. Folstein MF, Breitner JCS: Language disorder predicts familial Alzheimer's disease. Johns Hopkins Med J 149:145-147, 1981

47. Kiloh LG: Pseudo-dementia. Acta Psychiat Scand 37:336-351, 1961

48. McHugh PR, Folstein MF: Psychopathology of dementia: Implications for neuropathology, in Katzman R (ed): Congenital and Acquired Cognitive Defects, New York, Raven Press, 1979, pp 17-30

49. Lipowski ZJ: Delirium: Acute Brain Failure in Man. Springfield, Charles C Thomas, 1980, pp 14-15

50. Moruzzi, G Magoun HW: Brain stem reticular formation and activation of the EEG. Electroencephalog and Clin Neurophysiol 1:455-473, 1949

51. Victor M, Adams RD, Collins GH: The Wernicke-Korsakoff Syndrome. Philadelphia, F A Davis, 1971, p 4

52. Victor M, Adams RD, Collins GH: The Wernicke-Korsakoff Syndrome. Philadelphia, F A Davis, 1971, pp 166-170

53. Hunter R, Macalpine I: Three Hundred Years of Psychiatry 1535-1860. London, Oxford University Press, 1963, pp 406-407

54. Griesinger W: Mental Pathology and Therapeutics. New York, Hafner Press, 1965

55. Kraepelin E: Manic-Depressive Insanity and Paranoia. New York, Arno Press, 1976

56. Bleuler E: Dementia Praecox or the Group of Schizophrenias. New York, International Universities Press, 1950

57. Freud S: Psychoanalytic notes on an autobiographical account of a case of paranoia (dementia paranoides), in Strachey J (ed): The Standard Edition of the Complete Psychological Works of Sigmund Freud (vol 12). London, Hogarth Press, 1958, pp 9-82

58. Freud S: Mourning and melancholia, in Strachey J (ed): The Standard Edition of the Complete Psychological Works of Sigmund Freud (vol 14). London, Hogarth Press, 1957, pp 243-258

59. Meyer A: Substitutive activity and reaction-types, in Lief A (ed): The Commonsense Psychiatry of Dr. Adolf Meyer. New York, McGraw-Hill, 1948, pp 193-206

60. Jaspers K: Eifersuchtswahn, Ein Beitrag zur Frage: "Entwicklung einer Persönlichkeit oder Prozess." Zentralblatt für die Gesamte Neurologie und Psychiatrie 1:567-673, 1910

61. Winokur G, Clayton PJ, Reich T: Manic Depressive Illness. St Louis, C V Mosby, 1969, p 68

62. Bunney WE Jr, Hartmann EL, Mason JW: Study of a patient with 48-hour manic-depressive cycles. II. Strong positive correlation between endocrine factors and manic defense patterns. Arch Gen Psychiatry 12:619-625, 1965

63. Folstein SE, Folstein MF, McHugh PR: Psychiatric syndromes in Huntington's disease, in Chase TN (ed): Advances in Neurology (vol 23). New York, Raven Press, 1979, pp 281-289

64. Michael RP, Gibbons JL: Some inter-relationships between the endocrine system and neuropsychiatry. Int Rev Neurobiology 5:243-302, 1963

65. Quetsch RM, Achor RWP, Litin EM, Faucett RL: Depressive reactions in hypertensive patients. Circulation 19:366-375, 1959

66. Schildkraut JJ: Neuropsychopharmacology and the Affective Disorders. Boston, Little, Brown, 1969, pp 7-37

67. Kallmann F: Heredity in Health and Mental Disorder. New York, W W Norton, 1953, pp 128-129

68. Winokur G, Clayton PJ, Reich T: Manic Depressive Illness. St Louis, C V Mosby, 1969, pp 122-125

69. Slavney PR, Rich GB, Pearlson GD, McHugh PR: Phencyclidine abuse and symptomatic mania. Biol Psychiatry 12:697-700, 1977

70. Bunney WE Jr., Goodwin FK, Murphy DL, et al: The "switch process" in manic-depressive illness. II. Relationship to catecholamines, rem sleep and drugs. Arch Gen Psychiatry 27:304-309, 1972

71. Schneider K: Clinical Psychopathology (rev ed 5). New York, Grune and Stratton, 1959, pp 132-135

72. Mellor CS: First rank symptoms of schizophrenia. Br J Psychiatry 117:15-23, 1970

73. Slater E, Roth M: Clinical Psychiatry (ed 3). Baltimore, Williams and Wilkins, 1969, plate viii

74. Davison K, Bagley CR: Schizophrenia-like psychoses associated with organic disorders of the central nervous system: A review of the literature, in Herrington RN (ed): Current Problems in Neuropsychiatry (British Journal of Psychiatry Special Publication No 4). Ashford, Kent, Royal Medico-Psychological Association, 1969, pp 113-184

75. Pearlson GD, Veroff AE, McHugh PR: The use of computed tomography in psychiatry: Recent applications to schizophrenia, manic-depressive illness and dementia syndromes. Johns Hopkins Med J 149:194-202, 1981

76. Connell PH: Amphetamine Psychosis (Maudsley Monograph No 5). London, Chapman and Hall, 1958

77. Griffith JD, Cavanaugh J, Held J, et al: Dextroamphetamine: Evaluation of psychotomimetic properties in man. Arch Gen Psychiatry 26: 97-100, 1972

78. Snyder SH, Banerjee SP, Yamamura HI, Greenberg D: Drugs, neurotransmitters and schizophrenia. Science 184:1243-1253, 1974

79. Crow TJ: Molecular pathology of schizophrenia: More than one disease process? Br Med J 280:66-68, 1980

80. Heston LL: Psychiatric disorders in foster home reared children of schizophrenic mothers. J Ment Science 112:819-825, 1966

81. Kety SS, Rosenthal D, Wender PH, et al: Mental illness in the biological and adoptive families of adoptive individuals who have become schizophrenic: A preliminary report based on psychiatric interviews, in Fieve RR, Rosenthal D, Brill H (eds): Genetic Research in Psychiatry. Baltimore, Johns Hopkins University Press, 1975, pp 147-165

82. Allport GW: Personality. New York, Henry Holt, 1937, pp 65-85

83. Galton F: Measurement of character. Fortnightly Rev 42:179-185, 1884

84. Fancher RE: Pioneers of Psychology. New York, W W Norton, 1979, p 254

85. Watson RI: The Great Psychologists. Philadelphia, J B Lippincott, 1963, pp 308-315

86. Fancher RE: Pioneers of Psychology. New York, W W Norton, 1979, p 264

87. Piercy M: Testing for intellectual impairment—some comments on the tests and the testers. J Ment Sci 105:489-495, 1959

88. Terman LM, Oden MH: The Gifted Child Grows Up. Stanford, Stanford University Press, 1947, pp 377-378

89. Galton F: English Men of Science. London, Macmillan, 1974, p 12

90. Fulker DW, Eysenck HJ: Nature and nurture: Heredity, in Eysenck HJ (ed): The Structure and Measure of Intelligence. Berlin, Springer-Verlag, 1979, pp 102-132

91. Tuddenham RD: Soldier intelligence in World Wars I and II. Am Psychologist 3:54-56, 1948

92. Wheeler LR: A comparative study of the intelligence of East Tennessee mountain children. J Educat Psychol 33:321-334, 1942

93. Garber H, Heber FR: The Milwaukee project: Indications of the effectiveness of early intervention in preventing mental retardation, in Mittler P (ed): Research to Practice in Mental Retardation (vol. 1), Care and Intervention, Baltimore, University Park Press, 1977, pp 119-127

94. Butcher HJ: Human Intelligence: Its Nature and Assessment. London, Methuen, 1968, p 271

95. Clarke AM, Clarke ADB: Criteria and classification of subnormality, in Clarke AM, Clarke ADB (eds): Mental Deficiency (ed 3). New York, Free Press, 1974, p 15

96. Kushlick A, Blunden R: The epidemiology of mental subnormality, in Clarke AM,

Clarke ADB (eds): Mental Deficiency (ed 3). New York, Free Press, 1974, p 36

97. Penrose LS: The Biology of Mental Defect (ed 3). London, Sidgwick and Jackson, 1963, pp 49-50

98. Jacobs PA, Glover TW, Mayer M, et al: X-linked mental retardation: A study of 7 families. Am J Med Genetics 7:471-489, 1980

99. Weisz JR, Yeates KO: Cognitive development in retarded and nonretarded persons: Piagetian tests of the similar structure hypothesis. Psycholog Bull 90:153-178, 1981

100. Corbett JA: Psychiatric morbidity and mental retardation, in James FE, Snaith RP (eds): Psychiatric Illness and Mental Handicap. London, Gaskell Press, 1979, pp 11-25

101. Burger PC, Vogel FS: The development of the pathologic changes of Alzheimer's disease and senile dementia in patients with Down's syndrome. Am J Pathology 73:457-468, 1973

102. Reid AH: Psychoses in adult mental defectives: I. Manic-depressive psychosis. Br J Psychiatry 120:205-212, 1972

103. Bortner M, Birch HG: Cognitive capacity and cognitive competence. Am J Mental Def 74:735-744, 1970

104. Lazare A, Klerman GL, Armor DJ: Oral, obsessive and hysterical personality patterns. J Psychiat Res 7:275-290, 1970

105. Diagnostic and Statistical Manual of Mental Disorders (ed 3). Washington, American Psychiatric Association, 1980, pp 313-315

106. Jaspers K: General Psychopathology. Chicago, University of Chicago Press, 1963, p 443

107. Kretschmer E: A Text-Book of Medical Psychology. London, Oxford University Press, 1934, p 195

108. Presly AS, Walton HJ: Dimensions of abnormal personality. Br J Psychiatry 122:269-276, 1973

109. Mann AH, Jenkins R, Cutting JC, Cowen PJ: The development and use of a standardized assessment of abnormal personality. Psycholog Med 11:839-847, 1981

110. Slavney PR, McHugh PR: The hysterical personality: An attempt at validation with the MMPI. Arch Gen Psychiatry 32:186-190, 1975

111. Allport GW, Odbert HS: Trait-names: A psycholexical study. Psycholog Monographs 47:(Whole No 211), 1936

112. Eysenck HJ: Dimensions of Personality. London, Routledge and Kegan Paul, 1947

113. Eysenck HJ: Dimensions of Personality. London, Routledge and Kegan Paul, 1947, pp 246-247

114. Messick S: The standard problem: Meaning and values in measurement and evaluation. Am Psychol 30:955-966, 1975

115. Costa PT Jr, McCrae RR: Still stable after all these years: Personality as a key to some issues in adulthood and old age, in Baltes PB, Brim OG (eds): Life Development and Behavior (vol 3). New York, Academic Press, 1980, pp 65-102

116. Endler NS, Magnusson D: Personality and person by situation interactions, in Endler NS, Magnusson D (eds): Interactional Psychology and Personality. New York, John Wiley, 1976, p 1

117. Bridger WH, Birns BM, Blank M: A comparison of behavioral ratings and heart rate measurements in human neonates. Psychosomat Med 27:123-134, 1965

118. Shields J: Heredity and psychological abnormality, in Eysenck HJ (ed): Handbook of Abnormal Psychology. San Diego, Robert R Knapp, 1973, pp 565-571

119. Mischel W: On the interface of cognition and personality: Beyond the person-situation debate. Am Psychol 34:740-754, 1979

120. Finlay-Jones R, Brown GW: Types of stressful life event and the onset of anxiety and depressive disorders. Psycholog Med 11:803-815, 1981

121. Lader M, Marks I: Clinical Anxiety, New York, Grune and Stratton, 1971, p 8

122. Dohrenwend BP, Dohrenwend BS, Gould MS, Link B, Neugebauer R, Winch-Hitzig R: Mental Illness in the United States: Epidemiological Estimates. New York, Praeger, 1980

123. Frank JD: Persuasion and Healing (rev ed). Baltimore, Johns Hopkins University Press, 1980, pp 315-317

124. Eisenberg L: What makes persons "patients" and patients "well"? Am J Med 69:277-286, 1980

125. Slater E: The neurotic constitution: A statistical study of two thousand neurotic soldiers. J Neurology and Psychiatry 6:1-16, 1943

126. Freud S: Project for a scientific psychology, in Strachey J (ed): The Standard Edition of the Complete Psychological Works of Sigmund Freud (vol 1). London, Hogarth Press, 1957, pp 296-297

127. Freud S: Instincts and their vicissitudes, in Strachey J (ed): The Standard Edition of the Complete Psychological Works of Sigmund Freud (vol 14). London, Hogarth Press, 1957, pp. 121-123

128. Kinsey AC, Pomeroy WB, Martin CE: Sexual Behavior in the Human Male. Philadelphia, W B Saunders, 1948, p 638

129. Jaspers K: General Psychopathology. Chicago, University of Chicago Press, 1963, pp 323-324

130. Kallmann FJ: Comparative twin study on the genetic aspects of male homosexuality. J Nerv Ment Dis 115:283-297, 1952

131. Heston LL, Shields J: Homosexuality in twins; a family study and a registry study. Arch Gen Psychiatry 18:149-160, 1968

132. Slater E, Cowie V: The Genetics of Mental Disorders. Oxford, Oxford University Press, 1971, p 121

133. Lange J: Crime and Destiny. New York, Charles Boni, 1930, pp 45-46

134. Christiansen KO: Crime in a Danish twin population. Acta Genet Med Gemellol 19:323-326, 1970

135. Rosanoff AJ, Handy LM, Plesset IR: The Etiology of Child Behavior Difficulties, Juvenile Delinquency and Adult Criminality with Special Reference to Their Occurrence in Twins. Psychiatric Monograph (California) No 1, Sacramento, Department of Institutions, 1941.

136. Hutchings B, Mednick SA: Registered criminality in the adoptive and biological parents of registered male adoptees, in Mednick SA, Schulsinger F, Higgins J, Bell B (eds): Genetics, Environment and Psychopathology. Amsterdam, Elsevier/North-Holland, 1974, pp 215-227

137. Bleuler M: Familial and personal background of chronic alcoholics, in Diethelm O (ed): Etiology of Chronic Alcoholism. Springfield, Charles C Thomas, 1955, pp 110-166

138. Goodwin DW, Schulsinger F, Hermansen L, et al: Alcohol problems in adoptees raised apart from alcoholic biological parents. Arch Gen Psychiatry 28:238-243, 1973

139. Cadoret RJ, Cain CA, Grove WM: Development of alcoholism in adoptees raised apart from alcoholic biologic relatives. Arch Gen Psychiatry 37:561-563, 1980

140. Zinberg NE, Harding WM: Control over Intoxicant Use: Pharmological, Psychological and Social Considerations. New York, Human Sciences Press, 1982, p 151

141. Durkheim E: Suicide: A Study in Sociology. Glencoe IL, Free Press, 1951

142. Glueck S, Glueck E: Unravelling Juvenile Delinquency. New York, The Commonwealth Fund, 1950

143. Money J, Tucker P: Sexual Signatures: On Being a Man or a Woman. Boston, Little Brown, 1975, pp 86-118

144. Bowlby J: The making and breaking of affectional bonds. I. Aetiology and psychopathology in the light of attachment theory. Br J Psychiatry 130:201-210, 1977

145. Money J, Ehrhardt AA: Man and Woman Boy and Girl. Baltimore, Johns Hopkins

University Press, 1972, pp 96-103

146. Money J, Ehrhardt AA: Man and Woman Boy and Girl. Baltimore, Johns Hopkins University Press, 1972, pp 108-114

147. Imperato-McGinley J, Peterson RE, Gautier T, Sturla E: Androgens and the evolution of male-gender identity among male pseudohermaphrodites with 5 α-reductase deficiency. New Eng J Med 300:1233-1237, 1979

148. Lorand S: Anorexia nervosa. Psychosomat Med 5:282-292, 1943

149. Skinner BF: About Behaviorism. New York, Alfred A Knopf, 1974

150. Chomsky N: Review of BF Skinner's Verbal Behavior. Language 35:26-58, 1959

151. James W: The Principles of Psychology (vol 1). New York, Henry Holt, 1923, pp 291-342

152. Eysenck HJ: The Psychology of Politics. London, Routledge and Kegan Paul, 1963

153. Kelly GA: The Psychology of Personal Constructs (vol 1), A Theory of Personality. New York, W W Norton, 1955

154. Beck AT: Cognitive Therapy and the Emotional Disorders. New York, International Universities Press, 1976

155. Pilowsky I: Abnormal illness behaviour. Br J Med Psychol 42:347-351, 1969

156. Breuer J, Freud S: On the psychical mechanism of hysterical phenomena: Preliminary communication, in Strachey J (ed): The Standard Edition of the Complete Psychological Works of Sigmund Freud (vol 2). London, Hogarth Press, 1955, p 7

157. Sullivan HS: Clinical Studies in Psychiatry. New York, W W Norton, 1956, p 238

158. Freud S: The psychopathology of everyday life, in Strachey J (ed): The Standard Edition of the Complete Psychological Works of Sigmund Freud (vol 6). London, Hogarth Press, 1960

159. Foucault M: Madness and Civilization: A History of Insanity in the Age of Reason. New York, Pantheon, 1965, pp 3-7

160. Szasz TS: The Myth of Mental Illness: Foundations of a Theory of Personal Conduct (rev ed). New York, Harper and Row, 1974

161. Smith EE, Medin DL: Categories and Concepts. Cambridge, Harvard University Press, 1981

Index